How to Use Leverage
to Make Money
in Local Real Estate

George Bockl

D1252152

Englewood Cliffs, N.J.   PRENTICE-HALL, INC.

Reward Edition . . . . . April, 1973

Eighth Printing . . . . . July, 1979

PRINTED IN THE UNITED STATES OF AMERICA

43622—B&P

How to Use Leverage

to Make Money

in Local Real Estate

Dynamic Ideas
and a Little Money
Make Real Estate Fortunes

This book is for ambitious men who have little money but big ideas, because it demonstrates how ideas create fortunes in real estate. I offer detailed facts in narrative form showing, for instance, how I acquired a million dollar industrial building without a dollar of my own; how by recasting an eighteen year to a thirty year mortgage, I increased the value of an office building by $300,000; how an entrepreneur, wise in the ways of mortgage financing, bought a 200 apartment project for $2,350,000, and without investing a dime of his own, developed a tax protected $25,000 a year cash income.

Putting properties to their highest and best use

Hundreds of thousands of dollars can be made by putting properties to their highest and best use. Giving old buildings new uses offers golden opportunities for fortune building. Creatively remodeling old empty buildings and matching them with logical tenants can bring fantastic profits.

Among the many illustrations of how big money can be made from old buildings is the story of a Gay Nineties vintage office building which I bought for $65,000 with $5,000 down. By inexpensively remodeling it in a manner that preserved the old charm, I brought its rent up to $50,000 a year with an expenditure of only $35,000. After netting $25,000 a year for twelve years, I sold it for $225,000.

Merchandising the charm of old buildings is both an art and a science. It's spending $500 to modernize a lobby instead of $20,000 and still getting the same rent result. It means converting unused, dust laden garret space into a ballet studio, getting artists to clamor for Gothic windows which had hitherto been boarded up to hide dead storage space. It's grafting new ideas on old buildings and sky-rocketing their values. It's the art of converting minuses into pluses.

There's money in joining hands with government

Knowing how to cooperate with government can help you make a fortune. Government needs the help of private enterprise and private enterprise needs the help of government, if urban renewal is to rebuild our cities.

Government can help you acquire land through eminent domain, provide money at low interest rates and offer real estate tax freezes if you can come up with feasible projects that make sense. For instance, because the City of West Allis, Wisconsin, was willing to provide land for parking, I was able to build a $1,500,000 motor hotel in the heart of its business district. It was a case of private and public enterprise joining hands to create wealth. One could not have done it without the other.

Leasing existing buildings: a way to profit

Leasing existing buildings is one of the easy ways to get into big deals with little money. I obtained control of a $500,000 downtown building with no money of my own (see Chapter IV). The deal ended happily with an increase of $20,000 a year for the lessor, $22,500 a year for the lessee and a new lease on life for an old building.

A candy manufacturer didn't know what to do with a vacant 120,000 square foot loft building. I knew what to do with it but didn't have the money to buy it. I leased it for ninety-nine years. With $75,000 worth of face lifting and several tenant-attracting ideas, I added $150,000 of new value to the building.

How I sold $200,000,000 of real estate

How are the dynamic ideas that sell real estate reduced to practical specifics? I describe the techniques which my company used to sell $200,000,000 worth of real estate—the equivalent of selling every home, factory, office building and hotel in a typical town of 75,000. I show how I applied the ideas of thirty-day listings, second mortgage financing, "horizontal condominiums" and trading, to launch my real estate firm into orbit. And how, through profit sharing, stock distribution, health, accident, and life insurance programs, I built both the image and actuality of a dependable real estate institution.

Fortunes can be made in real estate of tomorrow

Just as the medical profession must assume the responsibility for the medical breakthroughs of tomorrow, so must the real estate profession solve the problems of better living tomorrow. We have gone a long way from caves to cathedrals to skyscrapers. But we must go on—not necessarily to make shelter more complex, but to make it more pleasant. I suggest that the wave of the future is in wildwood villages, villages in the sky, downtown malls, leisure clubs, Old McDonald's Little Farms, lighted golf courses and overnight hostels along secondary roadways next to highways, to cater to those who may want to hike, bicycle or use the horse and buggy the way our great-great-grandfathers did. I suggest a return to the small towns as a means of arresting the dehumanizing effects of an ant hill society.

Be alert for the "once in a lifetime deal"

Are you on the lookout for the "once in a lifetime deal"? A $12,000 a year restaurant manager took advantage of an unusual set of circumstances and made a quarter of a million dollars in one year—more than he could have made in a lifetime of managing restaurants. I describe how I passed up a "once in a lifetime deal" because of my faintheartedness, and let a million dollar profit from an office building trickle through my fingers. Because I was unable to bear the overwhelming stench that filled a tannery loft building, I passed it up, and provided the opening for a businessman with sturdier nostrils to buy it, disinfect it, lease it, and build a $100,000 annuity without investing any of his own money.

Host-guest management builds values

Management which aims for a host-guest relationship is not only gracious, it's practical. The importance of good management is grossly undervalued by investors. Often it makes or breaks a real estate investment. On rare occasions, such as the one I refer to in the Goldsmith Building in Chapter 3, unusual managerial skill not only can prevent a seventy-five year old building from slipping into the loft class, but can lift it to the exclusiveness of a high-toned medical building. This extraordinary stroke of imaginative management increased the value of the Goldsmith Building by $750,000. Incredible but true!

Pitfall investments—stay away

What are pitfall real estate investments? I bought, remodeled, leased and managed a loft building for five years and failed to keep it in the black because I wasn't aware of tenants' flight from inner core blight to the outskirts. Not recognizing the importance of parking to renting office space, I blundered early in my career into making a foolish offer on an old office building. I show how I was saved by the owner's more foolish refusal. I show how cheap construction shortcuts can boomerang, how a "quick buck" philosophy leads to a "no buck" philosophy. I point up the little-regarded fact that inordinate ambition blurs vision and fogs reason, that grandstanding for the applause of success can be deadly.

I caution the small investor looking for high yield in old flats and rooming houses to watch out for the dynamics of changing communities. The characters of neighborhoods are changing faster than ever before, and a small investor's property can easily be caught up in an avalanche of a deteriorating environment, and overnight a high return can plummet to no return.

A cooperative luxury apartment project can have everything in its favor, but if it's not blended properly with the right environment, it can fail badly—as the owner of such a project in Chapter 8 could tell you.

Small multiple tenant office buildings away from downtown do not have a good long range investment future. There is too much gamble in short term leases and absentee management. It's difficult to maintain a good image of a small building and even more difficult to obtain tenants for it.

The importance of time and timing in building a real estate fortune

Building a real estate fortune is intricately connected with time and timing. The leverage principle of investment real estate tames time by telescoping it so that a fortune can be built in a few years instead of several generations. Good timing is doing something when an idea is ripe for action.

There is a time to build office buildings, a time to remodel lofts, a time to buy land and a time to build shopping centers. There is also a time not to do any of these. Developing an intuition for anticipating local trends is a prerequisite for good timing. A merchant bought several blocks of land at $50 a front foot in a suburban area, and sold them ten years later at $500 a front foot. He anticipated a trend. He bought it at the lowest point, and sold it at the highest. There is a time to buy, a time to build, and a time to sell. Good timing does not just happen. It's preceded by an anlysis of facts and thoughtful reasoning which together pave the way for whatever good luck that follows

The average ones make the millions

The Phi Beta Kappas and honor students get the good jobs and the average ones with drive make the fortunes. Seldom do scholars have the temperament to become millionaires. Generally, it is the ordinary men who make fortunes in developing land. In Chapter 10, I describe how an entrepreneur who barely made it through high school made a killing after he interested a group of men in buying a subdivision in the path of growth. A year later, he split a $300,000 profit with his "angels." I show how a $75 a week lathe operator who gave up his job to become a real estate broker, made $15,000 the first month on optioning a tract of land. It was more than he had made in three years working in the factory. A surge of excitement ran through him. He made the sky the limit and reached for it. In fifteen years of optioning, buying and developing thousands of acres, he built a five million dollar fortune.

Two brothers-in-law, one an unsuccessful draftsman and the other an average insurance salesman, made a science of land development and wound up multimillionaires by following a few simple rules of logic. Professors of mathematics, physics and literature may have far superior mental prowess, but it would take the lifetime salaries of several dozen professors to accumulate what these brothers-in-law did in a decade.

I show how a fortune can be amassed by building fifty to one hundred new apartments a year for ten years and keeping them for investment. In Chapter 10, I describe how two young men with lots of drive have done it. And as a variation to the new apartment building theme, I show how a young attorney, just barely getting by in his law practice, gave it up to make a science of buying existing apartments and built a fortune.

Creating wealth should be a means not an end

Unless we can temper our feverish activity with lofty ideals, the best we can hope for is to wind up sterile millionaires—comfortable nd indulging, but without a soothing idea that really satisfies the heart. I suggest that we, the men of action, should devote some of our money-making energies to solving the problems of our communities and the world. Making a fortune is meaningful only if it is used as a means to contribute to humanity's welfare and qualitatively enrich personal experience. We put ourselves to our highest and best use only if, as men of action, we create wealth not as an end in itself, but as a means of expressing our deepest and finest promptings of the heart.

I acknowledge with gratitude the assistance of Wade Mosby, whose professional touch in preliminary editing helped to make a vision a reality

Contents

dynamic ideas

and a little money

make real estate fortunes

1.

Ideas More Than Money
Make Millions in Real Estate

*$17,500 lays the foundation for
a $4,000,000 office building*

The time was 1946. GI's were coming back from the war.
Milwaukee could have used several thousand new apartments,
but because of the lack of enterprising builders and financing
know-how, they were not being built. It didn't take much
real estate know-how to see the possibilities in the Arden
Apartments when they were offered to me for $47,500.

The building consisted of only seven apartments but each
had 10 large rooms—ideal for conversion into small modern
apartments. The structure was about forty years old and sub-
stantially built. It was built in the "gingerbread" era when
fireplaces with beautifully decorated carved wood borders
were in vogue. The rooms were spacious, with high ceilings.
Shortly after the turn of the century, luxury-loving Milwaukeeans had considered them the last word in gracious living.

The building was now just a shabby shadow of its aristo-
cratic past. An elderly couple rattled around in one of the

huge apartments. A bachelor led a lonely life in another. The rest of the building served as a rooming house.

The hallways were redolent with 40 years of meals—cabbage evidently the favorite entree. Bare, low voltage, dust covered bulbs spread a dreary light inside the apartments. Oak floors which had gleamed elegantly in their heyday were now layered with greasy dirt. The walls had survived dozens of paintings and now had a final coat of grime.

I saw exciting potential in the building—but I had a money problem. I had too little of it. I overcame this handicap by substituting an idea for money. I suggested to a building and loan firm's secretary that he loan me $80,000. I would put down $17,500 in cash for the Arden, and the savings and loan association would advance a $30,000 first mortgage to pay the $47,500 to the seller. I then asked that he keep the mortgage open for another $50,000 to pay for remodeling the old Arden. The secretary was a little shaken by my effrontery until I showed him a layout of forty efficiency and one bedroom apartments with a rental projection of $40,000 a year. He was amazed, but agreed that facts were incontrovertible. It was a safe loan.

My next problem was to keep the remodeling costs from going beyond $50,000. If I could not, money would become a problem again. The trick was to preserve the old and economize on the new. I got along well until I fumbled my plastering contract with almost disastrous results.

I had hired a father, son and son-in-law team to do the plastering. Frankly, I did not ask whether they were union plasterers, but when the plastering union's business agent blared over the telephone that he wanted to see me, I knew I had a labor problem on my hands.

"What the hell's the matter with you, Bockl? Do you want a picket line around your building?" he yelled when I got to his office.

I assured him I didn't, and I was quick to point out that

I was using union labor for all of my other trades.

"I don't give a damn about your other trades. I'm interested in your plastering. Rip it down and get a union plasterer," he said furiously.

"You can't mean that," I said.

"I certainly do," he snorted.

"Look," I said, "I'm using union labor for all my other contracts, and with the shortage of plasterers I don't think I've committed such a terrible crime if the men I hired are not union. Besides, why don't you try to get them into your union instead of spending all your energies accusing me?" Then I changed my pace. "Haven't you ever made a mistake? O.K., let's say I've made one! It's not so terrible that I should have to rip the plaster down. There are dozens of GI's looking for apartments right now who would be needlessly delayed. Perhaps there's one in your own family."

"Yeah, my son," he agreed.

"Well," I said realizing that I struck pay dirt, "your son can have an apartment right now."

He gave me no further trouble. The conversion project was completed and forty GI families moved in. I specifically gave preference to GI's with children. The building soon was humming with young married couples whose offspring had either arrived or were en route.

The old gave way to the new in many ways. Young, eager people replaced the old men and women who used to sit in loneliness gazing out through dust-grimed windows. The old and new walls were painted in soft pastel colors. The grimy oak floors were sanded and stained, and gleamed richly under the diffused light of new electric fixtures. Old bathrooms were remodeled and new ones installed. Bright new kitchens were created out of old pantries, corners of living rooms, or halves of old bedrooms, and colorfully decorated by the young homemakers.

The gross rent, including all utilities, was $40,000 a year

and the net was $20,000. The $80,000 open end mortgage was closed, and a once marginal property now was worth about $175,000 based on its income.

The venture radiated its benefits to the seller, who had wanted to get rid of a "lemon"; to the savings and loan association which wound up with a safe loan, and to the tenants who were delighted to move into the newly remodeled apartments. But it was I who gained most of all, because I had the exhilarating experience of putting an old piece of real estate to its highest and best use and making more than a fair profit doing it.

The Arden Apartments conversion was not a spectacular project, but it turned out to be the key deal which laid the foundation for my $4,000,000 Bockl Building. With the $40,000 a year stream of income, I was able to pay off the mortgage in a few years so that in 1955, when my mind was beginning to turn to bigger things, I owned a free and clear property.

The $17,500 seed money which I invested in 1946 grew into a tall $200,000 equity by 1955. I began dreaming in my bolder moments that perhaps I could use the Arden Apartments as seed money for a multimillion dollar project. I was ripe for a new idea and I did not have long to wait.

Erecting an office building without an anchor tenant

In 1955, while I was attending a convention of building owners and managers in Denver, I saw two new buildings rising high above the smaller and older buildings of the city's 75 year old downtown section. They were the Mile High Center and the Denver Club building. These two new structures cast a stirring spell on the city—and on me. On my way home, the thought kept recurring: "If it can be done in Denver, why not in Milwaukee?"

By this time, I had acquired several paying properties in

Milwaukee, and might have been content to rest on my oars. But, bitten by the bug to build, I sold the Arden Apartments for $200,000 and began looking for a site. I found one that I thought was ideal. And then I had the first of many set-backs. The lessee of the property had an option to buy it, and did. Right under my nose.

With perhaps more determination than foresight, I paid $75,000 for a 100 by 120 foot lot at North 14th Street and West Wisconsin Avenue, eleven blocks from the center of town. It was a poor site for an office building. It was too small and was in Marquette University's congested student area. It was neither downtown nor away from it, but I was stuck with it. Or was I?

My lot adjoined a motion picture theater. I learned that the theater owner also owned a 200 by 300 foot lot at North 21st Street and West Wisconsin Avenue. I set up a logical deal for both of us. He needed my lot for parking. I wanted his for my building. I offered him my lot for the $75,000 I had put into it, and offered him $175,000 for his.

He was reluctant to sell. His lot was a beauty—away from downtown congestion, yet only five minutes from the center of town. My emphasis that he needed the 14th Street lot for parking for his theater patrons must have impressed him. We exchanged lots and I was on my way.

I engaged, or I should say "gambled on," Robert Rasche, a young architect, in the hope that he would pour his heart and soul into my building as a stepping stone for his career. With his beautifully colored rendering of the building, I began to solicit tenants for office space. There was interest. But I couldn't convert it into signed leases. When my first cousin, an orthopedic surgeon, refused to sign a lease in advance for fear that if I didn't get financing he might be out in the street, I realized that I had better get my financing first before spinning my wheels trying to get signed leases.

In ten months I was turned down by ten mortgage companies. It takes about a month of hard work to receive a final turndown because the machines of large insurance companies grind slowly. The reasons for my turndowns were all the same —"Get the tenants first—then we'll finance."

In the meantime I had spent $10,000 to remove several old shacks from the lot, and about $10,000 for preliminary plans.

Which came first, the chicken or the egg? This was an academic question no longer. I had to answer it, and the answer was: "Get financing first and the tenants will come later."

In desperation, but still unbowed, I went to the Mutual Savings and Loan Association in Milwaukee, a company which had never made a loan of over $500,000. Its president, eighty-two year old Joseph Crowley was interested in my plight. He was a self-made man who had been in situations similar to mine and had managed to extricate himself by creative thinking. We vibrated on the same wave length. He was in the mood for a financial fling. With his help, I persuaded his board of directors to lend me $2,800,000 on the following terms: $1,500,000 was to be paid out during the course of construction until I was 65% rented. If I failed to rent 65% of my office space by the time I used up the $1,500,000, they would take title to my Pereles office building and a 16 family apartment building, together worth about $325,000, and use the proceeds toward the deal. Since my $175,000 lot was free and clear, the mortgage company had a cushion of $500,000. In addition, the deal had all my contract handling, promotional, and leasing services—worth several hundred thousand dollars.

I started building and leasing—a race which, if to be successful, had to be won by the leasing.

The rate was $4 per square foot per year, including central air conditioning, heat, janitorial service, maintenance and daily cleaning. It did not include light or parking. My main selling points were:

"Don't let your secretary wilt in summer and endure drafts in winter. Have her enjoy central air conditioning to perk her up in summer and keep her comfortable in winter." This was the air conditioning theme. We showed a picture of a secretary perspiring at her typewriter, with a plant wilted over her desk, and another picture of the same secretary crisp and trim with the same wilted plant straightened and perked up.

We advertised our 400 parking stalls underneath the first two floors of the building by showing how a tenant could get from his car to his office desk in sixty seconds.

We illustrated how a $3 per square foot suite could cost more per month if poorly laid out (showing wasted area) than a $4 per square foot suite well planned and meeting the custom built needs of the tenant. We called this "intense space utilization."

We stressed that being 15 blocks from downtown was an asset and not a detriment. The building was only 5 minutes from the heart of town—yet away from its congestion.

Our advertising called attention to the trees and landscaping surrounding our proposed building.

My crucial experience was with General Motors. The local manager approved the layout I made for him. It fit his needs perfectly. The bay spacing was exactly what he wanted, but General Motors had never heard of George Bockl and the New York office was dragging its feet about signing. What if it signed and the building for one reason or another would not be completed in time?

I decided to go to New York and meet the man who held the decision in his hands—P. H. Robinson. He was to become the key in renting the building.

"I can't blame you for hesitating," I told him. "Your company has never heard of me. However, at some time in the dim past no one had heard of General Motors either. It was someone's faith in General Motors that enabled you to grow.

I ask you that you place the same faith in me that others at one time placed in you. Without this faith, businesses could never grow."

We hit it off well together. I realized that a huge corporation is as warm or as cold as its officials. General Motors, though a financial giant, became a warm human being in the form of "Pete" Robinson. Several weeks later General Motors signed a lease for 7,000 square feet.

Soon I had several other tenants signed, and I was on my way. I ran an advertising campaign in the financial section of the *Milwaukee Journal* which paid off. I started a series of ads with:

"There's a Good Reason Why General Motors Is Moving into the Bockl Building."

I featured a picture of the local manager with a quotation from him about why he was moving into the Bockl Building. Below I stressed my four main selling points: central air conditioning, intense space utilization, ample parking for tenants and clients, and five minutes to the center of town yet away from its congestion.

Among prospective tenants who were sitting on the fence were the Prudential Life Insurance Company of America, Aluminum Company of America, Mutual Life Insurance Company of New York, and others. One by one they signed up, and as each signed, I repeated the headline in my ad, "There's a Good Reason Why etc." using the name of the new tenant.

Selling office space in Milwaukee is different and more difficult than selling it in New York or Chicago. Where in those cities space is rented by the 10,000 to 50,000 square feet, in Milwaukee it is rented by the 1,000 to 5,000 square feet. That is why it is so much more difficult to build in the small cities. There are fewer large anchor tenants to be obtained.

I signed about 65 leases before I was 65% rented. By a near miracle, that 65% point arrived at about the same time I had used up all of the $1,500,000 in payments to my contractors.

When I appeared before the board of the Mutual Savings and Loan Association for the $1,300,000 balance of the loan, they at first feigned reluctance, but soon burst out in warm approval of my progress. The 82 year old Mr. Crowley was beaming as much as I was. In a way, we were both in it together. He had put his money and judgment on my inspiration and effort, and at this moment we both looked good.

Needless to say, the last 35% rented much faster than the first 65%. In fact, by the time I was 100% rented, there were prospective tenants for 30,000 more square feet.

An idea that started at a convention in Denver built a building. It took faith—or a strong belief that there was a need to be met, and a little courage to see it through.

I have learned to allow things to unfold harmoniously—a rose opens up more beautifully and naturally when you give it time than if you try to open its petals prematurely. My inability to buy one lot and my mistake in purchasing another were two failures that turned out to be two necessary stepping stones. Had I pushed too hard to build on either of the first two lots, I might have failed.

Faith and work are an unbeatable combination. Faith gave me the courage and stamina to make 1,000 personal calls to obtain 103 tenants for the Bockl Building. And now, with little more than the original $17,500 seed money I had planted in the Arden Apartments, and which I harvested and replanted in the Bockl Building, I can gratefully say that my equity position has grown to $1,500,000 if I place a conservative value of $4,000,000 on the Bockl Building. My $1,500,000 equity was built from the $175,000 I invested in the lot, $225,000 in additional cash, $300,000 through mortgage reduction, and $800,000 in value increment. Ideas more than money make millions in real estate.

The crucial decision I had to make was exchanging a $20,000-a-year sure income from the Arden Apartments for the uncertainties of a $4,000,000 project. It was an agonizing decision. But there is no way to grow without risks. In making my decision, money considerations were important, but deeper motivations were involved. I can say I was almost driven to give up my security for an opportunity to express my real estate creativity in a new and bigger dimension. I like to feel that I had the urge of the artist. My challenge was to meet the needs of commercial tenants in a way they had never been met before. Going from the known to the unknown has fascinated men in all sorts of activities and it is not surprising that it should fascinate me—the fascination of creating the first modern office building in a metropolitan area of a million people.

Risk-taking is not for the overly cautious, hand-wringing men who fear failure. It is for those who plan well, work hard, and are ready to fail if their best is not enough. The creative man must learn how to fail gracefully and use success not as something to crow about but as a stepping stone for another round of activity. These thoughts are what prompted me to give up a $20,000-a-year secure income for life, for the excitement and risk of building the Bockl Building.

How I got on target on a shell factory

A real estate operator looking for a quick profit made a $75,000 deposit on a 200,000 square foot concrete industrial building. His offer was $475,000. He took a half year to close the deal, hoping to rent the space at 50 cents a square foot. He failed to rent the building and lost his $75,000 deposit.

With these facts as a backdrop, a persuasive broker induced me to meet with the owner of this building, who used part of it for shell manufacturing. He now wanted to sell for

$400,000. We chatted amicably for several minutes and then I asked him to show me his shell manufacturing operation. During the course of my inspection, the owner said ruefully that manufacturing machine gun shells was a risky business—the government could cancel out with only thirty days notice. This gave me an idea.

I said, "How would you like to get a ten year lease on the space you need for manufacturing shells with a clause allowing you to cancel the lease at the same time the government cancels its order to manufacture shells? This is like having your cake and eating it too."

"I think I would be interested in such a lease," he said. "What's the gimmick?"

"I don't like to call it a gimmick," I said. "Let's call it a creative idea which would permit you to run your lucrative shell business and yet be able to cancel your lease obligation when your orders are cancelled. But in giving you this leeway, I would like to have something in return. Sell me your building for $250,000 instead of the $400,000 you're asking. From what I gather, if you have two or three good years in the shell manufacturing business, the $150,000 difference would be more than offset by the cancelable lease I'm ready to give you."

"You've got a good idea there," he said with growing interest. "I'll let you know in a few days."

A month later I owned the building for $250,000. The ex-owner leased 30,000 square feet of the first and second floors for ten years at 75 cents a square foot, with a thirty day cancellation clause.

I leased another 90,000 square feet to the Gleason Corporation, for ten years at $35,000 a year before the deal was closed. On the strength of these two leases, I was able to obtain a $225,000 loan. I still had 80,000 square feet to rent.

The Cutler-Hammer, Inc., plant practically surrounded this

building, yet the management never had shown any interest in it. I had a hunch that sooner or later a situation would develop where they might need some extra space. My hunch was right.

Five months after I bought the building, they communicated through their broker an interest in using part of the building for warehousing excess material. I rented the 80,000 square feet for $30,000 a year for three years with a two year option. My total yearly rental was $30,000 from Cutler-Hammer, $35,000 from the Gleason Corporation and $22,500 from the previous owner of the building for a total of $87,500 a year.

Five years passed. I was not sure whether Cutler-Hammer would renew its lease beyond its two year option. In the meantime, the shell manufacturing tenant had moved out and Gleason took over its space on the same terms, the lease expiring at the same time as Gleason's prime lease. This added value to the building. I decided it was a good time to sell, and that Cutler-Hammer was a far more logical owner of this building than I.

A creative idea made it possible for me to purchase the building at an attractive price and I knew I had to come up with an equally creative idea to make Cutler-Hammer want to buy it. This is what I "dreamed up," and it worked. As you will note, it made sense for both of us.

I called the Cutler-Hammer broker and told him that his client could buy the building for $365,000 without a down payment, and furthermore, I pointed out, the owner could meet all the fixed expenses plus the interest and principal payments on the mortgage from the $57,500 Gleason yearly rental. The fixed expenses consisted mainly of $13,000 in real estate taxes and $9,000 for heating. The balance of $35,500 of the Gleason rent could be applied on the mortgage for interest and principal. This meant that Cutler-Hammer would not have to pay the $30,000-a-year rent they were paying to me for their 80,000 square feet. But this wasn't all. I arranged for Cutler-Hammer to be able to expand its operations in the building by getting Gleason to agree to vacate its space any time during its lease if it got six months free rent. I got this in writing. And then I came up with the most telling argument of all. There was talk of an expressway cutting through a part of the Cutler-Hammer plant. Within several years the plant might need my entire building.

The Cutler-Hammer broker did an excellent job of conveying the information to the president of Cutler-Hammer. The deal was made on the terms I outlined. Cutler-Hammer subsequently paid the six months free rent bonus to Gleason and took over the entire building.

The deal was a favorable one for me because, although I did not receive any down payment, my equity between the $365,000 selling price and the 125,000 mortgage balance was bankable, since Cutler-Hammer is one of the 500 largest corporations in the country. I also felt that after the deal was made, there would be a good chance of getting paid out. My hunch was right. Within six months I received all of my cash.

The $25,000 seed money I planted in the shell factory brought a generous $175,000 profit. It's axiomatic that when a real estate developer makes a profit he becomes ripe for another deal. It's a time when his mind becomes magnetized for action, and if he is not too careful he can be drawn into a venture that needs a second and third look. I was no exception. Within several months my profit began burning a hole in my pocket, and I got into one of the most unique deals of my life.

Converting a warehouse into a
first-class medical building

In 1925 a prominent Milwaukee family built a warehouse on Prospect Avenue, a street which 35 years later developed into a prestige apartment district. In 1960 the 100,000 square

foot warehouse was woefully mislocated both for the owner
and residents in the neighborhood. The owner put the building on the market for $500,000. There were no takers. The
price dropped to $400,000, and then $300,000, and still no
one found an answer for putting the structure to its highest
and best use.

I was teaching a course in Creative Real Estate at the
University of Wisconsin at the time and offered this building
as a problem to my students. One said it ought to be converted to a nurses' dormitory because it was close to two large
hospitals. Another student suggested it be converted to apartments to blend in with the neighborhood. Still another thought
the warehouse ought to be razed and a brand-new luxury
apartment built because the site was only a block from Lake
Michigan and merited the highest development. Then one student hit the jackpot. He said that since Prospect Avenue was
zoned residential and since the warehouse was the only piece
zoned commercial, that it ought to be converted to a medical
center catering to the doctors of the two nearby hospitals.
As soon as he said it, he rang a bell in my mind. It was a case
of the pupil teaching the teacher. The more I thought of it
during the weeks that followed, the more convinced I became
he was right. I bought the warehouse for $205,000.

Converting a warehouse into a medical center presents
many more problems than building a new building. In planning a new project one does not inherit the limitations of an
existing structure. But this was only the beginning of my problems. The more formidable ones were ascertaining the cost of
remodeling, mortgaging it without knowing costs in advance,
setting up a rental schedule and rental promotion, creating
parking, and perhaps, the most important of all, removing the
warehouse look and giving it the clean, attractive appearance
that a medical center should have.

The problem of ascertaining the cost of remodeling was

almost insurmountable. There were only a half dozen windows in the entire building. The inside was a labyrinth of dimly lit passageways dotted with steel doors behind which were stored furniture, antiques, memorabilia, and sentimental if not valuable possessions of many well-known Milwaukee families. There were few heating and plumbing lines and only inadequate electric wiring in the building. The exterior was of a white glazed tile that was badly cracked and discolored on the first two floors, and for some reason, in pretty good condition for the upper four floors. Since I had no idea whether I was going to fill the entire building with physicians, or a combination of doctors and other commercial tenants, there was no way of determining the costs in advance. I decided on a bold plan of action which required eye-ball to eye-ball negotiation with my key contractors on the basis of time and material with an agreed upon margin of profit. This is dangerous at best. I don't recommend it. But I had no choice. It was that type of deal.

Financing a conversion without knowing the cost in advance cannot be arranged with an ordinary mortgage man—he has to be extraordinary. After being turned down by a half dozen ordinary men, I was fortunate enough to be introduced to Jim Gibson, a mortgage representative of The John Hancock Insurance Company, whose Milwaukee mortgage correspondent was The Richter-Schroeder Company. I told Mr. Gibson that I had no tenants and that I could only guesstimate the cost of remodeling at about $1,100,000. However, I pointed out to him, I had the finest location for a medical center, and that there were no other commercial sites that could be zoned in the near future to compete against me.

I said to him, "If you're looking for a mortgage wrapped in a blue ribbon, safe and cut and dried, to which any ordinary man can say yes, then this is not it. However, if you're willing to dream with me, risk with me, and back me on a real estate adventure that will not only meet a need but could revitalize a neighborhood, then we will both be doing the extraordinary. In an adventure such as this, I need an imaginative mortgage man like I hope you are, and you need an entrepreneur like me. Together we can do the unusual."

After three hours of exhilarating negotiation which often bordered on the inspirational, he agreed to make an $850,000 loan. But because the mortgage was a bit more risky than the usual, he upped the interest rate to 6¼ per cent. I didn't object. He was entitled to it. It was not a mill run loan.

In retrospect the thought of expecting a doctor to look at an old warehouse and sign a lease on the basis of a word picture of what his offices would look like, staggers me now. But it didn't scare me then. My optimistic enthusiasm melted all doubts. I had a tremendous talking point: I was only one block from one hospital and eight blocks from another. Over 500 doctors were within walking distance of my building! This was my key argument in presenting the evidence to substantiate the $850,000 mortgage. Of course, I did not fail to mention to prospective tenants that I had satisfied the exacting needs of thirty-five doctors in the Bockl Building, and based on that record, they had good reason to rely on me for similar results.

A former chief of staff of St. Mary's Hospital, with a group of four other surgeons, cautiously explored the possibility of moving their clinic, located three miles away from St. Mary's Hospital, to my building. As I had anticipated, they were enchanted with being one block from their base of operations. They were hesitant about leasing space they hadn't seen. I pointed out that I had never seen them operate, either, but that if the occasion arose, I would be willing to have any of them operate on me. Why not some mutual confidence? This argument apparently had results. After more negotiations, they signed a lease.

This was the beginning of an avalanche. Doctors have a way of following other doctors, especially those with good reputations. I filled about half the building with medical men, and the other half with commercial and professional tenants. When top flight lawyers and insurance companies offered to lease space in my building, I decided to take them instead of waiting and risking failure to fill the entire building with medical tenants. I leased part of the ground floor to a Big Boy Restaurant with a $600 a month minimum against 5 per cent of the gross, and after the first year of operation, I was receiving close to $20,000 a year rent from the restaurant. It was a pleasant financial surprise—a bonanza for me and a boon to my tenants who were delighted with its food, convenience, and pleasant atmosphere.

Creating ample parking was important. I solved it this way. Next to the warehouse and included in the real estate I purchased, was a one-story service garage of approximately 13,000 square feet. I removed the roof and added three tiers of parking. It provided about 130 parking stalls, enough for the all day parking needs of the tenants in the building, and for the transient parking of the patients and clients who came to see them.

Function without aesthetics is like a body without a soul. Removing the warehouse look and creating a handsome structure without spending too much money was an economic as well as an architectural challenge. We solved it this way: the building was of a triangular shape. One of its angles nosed into the corner of Prospect and North Avenues. We snipped off a piece of this angle on the first floor and converted it into a lovely Japanese garden, and made it a part of the lobby. Since the white tiles on the first two floors were broken and discolored, I had them covered with new white-painted brick, and picture framed the brick with a black, ten-inch iron border. The exterior of the upper four floors was of brick and tile, and in good condition. I had it painted white to match the lower two floors. The result was a dazzling white structure that looked brand new.

Within 18 months after remodeling started, I had the building 100 per cent occupied. The rent roll was $240,000 a year. The net before principal and interest payments was $120,000 a year, and the cash flow after mortgage amortization and interest was $50,000 a year. The building was appraised at $1,500,000. My cost was $1,300,000. It was a good deal—not a spectacular one.

The impact of this conversion, however, was spectacular. It sparked a neighborhood renewal program. Three new buildings were built in its wake and others began to pretty up and remodel. The warehouse eyesore which marred the residential tone of Prospect Avenue became a mark of beauty. The Big Ben Clock which was housed in a 10 foot high dome atop the warehouse and whose hands had not moved during the last 20 years, was repaired, painted white, and lit up so that people could read the time for blocks around. The doctors were the most appreciative tenants in the building because their offices were now only a few minutes away from their hospital. Many of them seldom used their cars; they walked to their hospital, and, being close to the lake and a park, it was a pleasant walk.

New wealth had been created through private urban renewal which made sense for the entrepreneur, created a safe $850,000 loan for an insurance company, increased the tax base for the city, and gave work to dozens of men for more than a year. Also it created a going business concern which sold $240,000 a year in services, paid out $190,000 a year in wages, taxes, and interest and principal mortgage payments, and left a fair profit to the entrepreneur who dreamed, risked, and made private urban renewal work.

2.

Urban Renewal – an Opportunity for a Challenging Partnership

If private enterprise pays lip service to urban renewal but does nothing about it unless there are quick profits to be made, government can be expected to jump into the real estate business. Admittedly, there are certain roles in urban renewal best suited to government—among them long range community planning, condemnation of entire blighted neighborhoods so that fresh starts may be made, and financing some of these vast projects. But private developers can play more of a role than merely being the not-so-loyal opposition. Renewal can be a challenge, and often a rewarding one, for the private developer. There is a third course toward urban renewal: a partnership between private and public enterprise. Not all of government is red tape bureaucracy, and not all private developers are money-hungry opportunists.

Moderates of both camps are attempting to remove some of the hurdles for private enterprise, and to hold back the bureaucrats who are champing at the bit to get going with public housing. Real estate and finance techniques to enable private and public enterprise to work together are being developed.

THE ROLE OF PRIVATE URBAN RENEWAL

There are several obstacles which make it difficult for private enterprisers to deal with urban renewal. Some of them are of their own making, others are real estate facts over which they have no control.

The problem of assembling land for a large project by private enterprise often is insurmountable. Selfish property owners so unreasonably obsessed with their own welfare that they completely disregard the good a project can do for their community can hopelessly wreck the best-intentioned projects. Again and again, I have seen a rugged individualist owner of a splinter of land in a square block stall a project by demanding a "hold up" price, and delaying things so long that the entrepreneur gives up in disgust. Some real estate men think they are "men of vision" when they buy up small parcels in strategic blocks and demand unconscionable prices when entrepreneurs attempt to assemble land for a project. I know of several cases where overly ambitious enterprisers "paid through the nose" for such splinters of real estate. In permitting costs to run out of hand, they caused their projects to fail.

Absentee ownership often proves an impediment to the private developer interested in urban renewal. A square block of downtown real estate may have as many as twenty owners, with perhaps half of them living outside of the city When word gets around that a private developer is interested in assembling land for a project, the absentee owners jack up their prices unrealistically and urban renewal is nipped in the bud.

In addition to the road blocks which private entrepreneurs set up against each other, the private developer is squeezed by three other factors: rising real estate taxes, high interest rates, and rising costs of construction.

Unless a private developer knows his "p's and q's" he can be so inundated in expense that all he gets to see is red—very little black. If rents would rise in proportion to costs, the entrepreneur would have a chance. Unfortunately, overbuilding plague soon sets in and holds rentals down. Many well-conceived projects are foundering today because of high vacancies or low rentals or both.

Another headache of private enterprise is the red tape connected with putting a project through City Hall. The developer often has many of his cherished ideas lopped off by the planning commission, public works committee or Common Council. Often his original plans become so enmeshed in tortuous red tape that an entirely different project emerges.

A spirited entrepreneur often gets discouraged when opinionated officials or myopic lay people in authority get so technical or officious that they make it impossible for him to go on. These hazards of democracy can be overcome by more enlightened thinking at the grass root level. We cannot afford to have projects fail because officials keep their eyes so glued to the trees that they lose sight of the forest.

In spite of all the impediments, private enterprise is making a contribution to renewing our cities. The less hardy, less imaginative and less able entrepreneurs are falling by the wayside. This is the way private enterprise works—in the classical manner. The fittest survive.

The Madison Inn—private urban renewal at its profitable best

A salesman who learned first-hand about the inadequacies and special amenities of motor hotels while he traveled from city to city, decided to build the ideal small hotel which would incorporate all the pluses and eliminate all the minuses of the dozens of hotels he had stayed in.

His search for a site and a city ended when he found an old rooming house on the corner of Francis and Langdon Streets in the heart of the University of Wisconsin campus in Madison. He was a top salesman and knew a great deal about his products, but he knew little about financing a motor hotel. For a full year he shuttled from one mortgage company to another without being able to breathe reality into his "dream." He received a dozen turndowns.

One day he came to my office and said, "George, I've got a terrific site for a motor hotel and some terrific ideas about how to build it, but nobody pays any attention to me. I can't get it financed. Give me a lift and you can be my partner."

There was no question about it. He picked the right city, the right location, and he had good ideas. There were two business generators which assured the hotel high occupancy. One was its location in the heart of the 20,000 student residential area on fraternity and sorority row. This meant that parents would be using its facilities when they visited their sons and daughters over weekends. The second and more important business generator was the Wisconsin Center, a University building used constantly for meetings and seminars. It was a half block from the site. The Wisconsin Center needed the hotel and the hotel needed the Wisconsin Center. When I checked into the project more carefully, I discovered that the University was considering putting a floor of rooms on top of the Wisconsin Center to accommodate its out-of-town seminar participants. Its spacious public areas were used by small and large special interest groups in business, education and religion. Its seminar participants came from many parts of the state and the Middle West. It was an excellent potential occupancy generator.

I went to the largest savings and loan association in Madison and suggested to the secretary that private enterprise had a golden opportunity to meet a need for a hotel. As persuasively as I knew how, I documented the two reasons why a seventy-five room motor hotel would be a success on our location. To add a human interest touch, I told him that my two daughters were attending the University of Wisconsin and how convenient it would be for my wife and me to stay there while visiting them. I didn't fail to mention that it would be convenient for thousands of other parents as well.

We obtained a 75 per cent loan and got the general contractor to agree to amortizing $60,000 of his contract over five years. This meant that we only had an investment of about 15 per cent in the project. This is excellent motorized hotel financing, but such mortgage terms are possible only when the project is unusually well conceived, when it has enough natural business generators to assure its success. The Madison Inn was one of those.

The Madison Inn is a success. It is enjoying over 80% occupancy. And I am happy to say that the parents visiting their sons and daughters and the Wisconsin Center seminars are the main reasons for its booming business. Not only has the project turned out to be a commercial success, but its architect, A. A. Tannenbaum, won an Honor Award from the Wisconsin Chapter of AIA for distinguished accomplishment in architecture in 1963.

The Madison Inn—and I have sold my interest in it—is a good example of private enterprise meeting a need in which all involved benefited; the city, the University, the entrepreneur, the savings and loan association, the contractors, and the workmen.

A new million-dollar facility now stands where an old decrepit rooming house used to be. It is private urban renewal at its profitable best.

The Riverwood Apartments—private urban renewal at its spiritual best

At Aspen, Colorado, where I was participating in a seminar on humanistic studies, businessmen, educators, and government officials were discussing the differences between a conservative and a liberal.

Toward the end of the discussion, a famed psychiatrist said, "Let's cut out the nonsense of the fine political definitions. When you get down to bedrock, the difference between the conservatives and the liberals is that the conservatives are comfortable and fight to protect their status quo, while the liberals are uncomfortable and agitate in order to become as comfortable as the conservatives. The battle between the conservatives and the liberals is a fight between the haves and the havenots, between the comfortable and the uncomfortable."

What does this have to do with private enterprise? It is this: builders with comfortable means, who wish to become more comfortable, build where there is the greatest opportunity for profit. There is not much profit in building for the elderly. That's why few builders are meeting their needs. The uncomfortable elderly, however, are pushing their liberal representatives to give them housing they can afford. The result —the creation of thousands of public housing units for the elderly.

In 1955, Mrs. Ida Witte, in charge of a Golden Agers group in Milwaukee, challenged me at one of our community's fund raising meetings with these words:

"You businessmen are blind to the needs of people. Everybody wants to build for General Motors, Prudential Life Insurance Company, and other high paying clients. No one wants to build for the elderly. You don't have to tell me why. There's not enough profit in it. What, then, is going to happen to the elderly, to you and me when we get older?

"If you will not find a way to do it," she went on, "the government will. The elderly are not going to continue to live in their squalid rooming houses, in empty homes too large for them, or in their children's houses overcrowded with grand-children."

She planted a seed. In 1959, I answered her challenge by building the Riverwood Apartments, consisting of 94 units, and voluntarily restricting tenants to sixty years of age and over. The location for this project was ideal, but what was on the land was an eyesore. The centerpiece was an old farmhouse that had been converted into a duplex. Several other dilapi-dated shacks were strewn over the landscape. An abandoned outhouse was the final symbol of age and decrepitude.

I paid $80,000 for this countrylike acre and a half at the bend of the Milwaukee River, away from the city's conges-tion, yet only one block from the bus line, five blocks from a shopping area, and close to about one hundred other apart-ments occupied by young couples and their children. I may have overpaid for the site, but I was convinced it was the best one in the city for my purpose.

Overlooking the river, high on a bluff and landscaped beau-tifully with grass, flowers, shrubbery and trees, the Riverwood is truly an architectural masterpiece. The exterior is of white brick and the private patios for each apartment are enclosed with black corrugated grillwork. It looks like a Louisiana-style motel.

The architect, Robert Kemp, certainly must have been in-spired by the project to have it come out so well. He said that as he was planning it he was thinking of his own widowed mother.

I risked $225,000 of my own equity money to build it. It cost $725,000. Obtaining a $500,000 first mortgage became an adventure in financing because the practical-minded savings and loan secretaries didn't want to risk their money on a project that catered to low income, old people. After half a dozen failures, I persuaded a secretary of a building and loan company to risk his firm's money on the basis that the project was so right and worthy that it deserved special treatment. He happened to be a devoutly religious man who was adventurous enough to think beyond the practical rules of his association. His name is Al Kliebhan, secretary of the St. Francis Savings and Loan Association. His decision turned out to be both practical and inspirational. It was a safe loan and it helped people.

The Riverwood was completed and occupied in June of 1960. The apartments were unique in many ways. I spent $10,000 for landscaping to add to the natural beauty of its location. I spent $50,000 for building special amenities, such as a library, a cozy restaurant, a recreation room furnished with tables and sofas large enough to seat 150 people, a hobby shop where the elderly could pursue their crafts, a commissary where they could buy their staple foods and drugs, a prayer room, and an area for a pool table and shuffle board court. The property manager was instructed to serve free coffee and cookies twice a week, and provide entertainment such as card parties, amateur skits by the talented elderly, special movies and lectures. The management took on the responsibility not only of maintaining the tenants' shelter but of providing interests to occupy their leisure time as well.

The effect on the senior citizens has been visibly inspiring. An immobile woman who had been pining away in loneliness was advised by her doctor to move to the Riverwood. She became so stimulated by the new atmosphere and by the people her own age that, several weeks after she moved in on a stretcher, she was up and around hobnobbing with her newfound friends. Other tenants, who had been rattling in large eight-room homes or in noisy, congested rooming houses, have found a firmer hold on their remaining years in the new "Riverwood atmosphere." Each apartment has a bright living room, a modern kitchen, a good-sized bedroom, and a private patio which, in the summer, they love best of all. The apartment and the new way of life come to $82 a month.

Any widow or widower with a pension of $125 a month can afford this apartment and the life free from loneliness that it offers. One energetic 75 year old woman told me that she had an old age pension of only $75 a month, but asked me not to worry about her ability to pay rent because, as she put it, "there are one-hundred apartments near by where newly married couples live and I am the most experienced baby sitter there is. All I need is $50 a month for food because we old people don't eat much. I can assure you I'll earn it." She did.

Every day of the week something is going on in the public area. Square dances, lectures, games, movies. The management is instructed to keep the elderly people active. It meets with a committee of tenants and provides those activities most in demand. The relationship is not a commercial landlord-tenant formality—it is a way of life.

Doctors have recommended that their elderly patients move to Riverwood. Several who were depressed and lonely in their large homes came to life again amidst Riverwood's wholesome activity. Instead of wasting their time in idle loneliness, waiting for their children's rare visits, they became absorbed in creative leisure. The elderly mix genially and sympathetically exchange bits of gossip and information about their children. They laugh and have fun.

This congregate living gives the elderly a new status. They are able to invite their children and grandchildren to have dinner with them in "their" restaurant. It gives many a new lease on life. This type of living is new to them and they like it. The 150 residents of Riverwood, averaging 69 years of age, are among the happiest elderly people in Wisconsin. At any rate, that's what many of my tenants are telling me.

What type of people are they? Nurses, a retired sea captain, teachers, tool and die makers, librarians, etc., whose average income is about $2,500 a year from social security, old age pensions, or small private incomes. They are depression-proof tenants, because most of them receive income for life.

As one tenant put it, "My rent, including all utilities, is about $1,000 a year. All I get is $2,000. What I must do is budget my eating expenses at $1,000 a year, and I am set for the rest of my life. Oh yes, health insurance would help."

How am I doing financially? Not too badly. I am earning about 8 per cent on my equity plus amortization of principal. One can do much better financing similar projects through FHA, where 90 per cent financing and 40 year amortization is available to a private entrepreneur, and 100 per cent financing and 40 year amortization to a non-profit organization.

But the return of enjoyable living for the tenants of Riverwood was beyond their expectations and mine. I have built more remuneratively for General Motors Corporation, Prudential Life Insurance Company, Massachusetts Mutual Life Insurance Company and others, but I have not received the inspirational rewards that I have in building for the elderly. It was a business experience with a spiritual bonus.

I highly recommend mixing business with caring for people. The two aims are highly compatible. I especially recommend it to those who want to strengthen the private enterprise system but who make the mistake of becoming too mesmerized by high profits, and then complain when government steps in with public housing to care for people whom they neglect.

I know of five other buildings which have been built for the elderly as a result of people being impressed by Riverwood.

There is only one way that private enterprise can keep the

government from building public housing for the elderly. That is to meet this need creatively. If private enterprise fails, I believe it is not fair to point fingers at the government. Someone has to do it!

I started with a quotation by a famed psychiatrist and I would like to conclude with one of my own:

"A true liberal is a man who is comfortable but who is willing to become uncomfortable to help the uncomfortable become more comfortable."

THE ROLE OF PUBLIC URBAN RENEWAL

In his book, *Beyond The Welfare State*, Gunnar Myrdal, world renowned Swedish economist, predicted that as economies of countries become more complex, the tug of war between private and public enterprise will become accentuated. Where private enterprise meets the needs of people, he says, it will keep public enterprise out. Where it fails, public enterprise will quickly fill the vacuum. And when public enterprise fails, private enterprise can roll it back if it uses initiative, imagination and efficiency. This tug of war, he contends, will continue in the indefinite future and will keep both of them on their toes.

Myrdal's theory is being demonstrated in urban renewal. Private enterprise is unable to provide housing for the low income groups at a profit and consequently it is not being built. Public enterprise has stepped in to fill the vacuum with public housing.

In 1948 the city of Milwaukee financed and built three projects, consisting of about a thousand apartment units, to meet the needs of veterans. Rentals were set at $55 per month for a one-bedroom apartment, $70 for a two-bedroom unit, and $75 for a three-bedroom. These prices were about 30 per cent below the prevailing rental market. Grateful veterans in the low income bracket appreciated this helpful and concrete welcome their city gave them when they came back from the war. And the city gave little away in meeting this housing need. It sold 40 year bonds at 3 per cent and is meeting its interest and principal obligations from the income of the projects. And it is paying 65 per cent of the normal real estate taxes as well. This is public enterprise at its finest.

Obviously private enterprise was unable to create housing at these low rents because it would have had to pay 6 per cent interest instead of the city's 3 per cent, it usually gets 20-25 year amortization instead of the city's 40 year, it has to pay more for land, and it has to bear the full real estate tax load.

Ideally, public urban renewal should be limited to the grass root level of government. Unfortunately, local level government can only meet the problems of the needy in a limited way. Where it cannot do the job alone, the federal government must step in and help. This has happened in Milwaukee, as it has happened in dozens of cities in America. In Milwaukee, 2000 apartments have been built with federal funds. These units cater to the very low income groups. The minimum rental is $34 per apartment. Other rentals vary in proportion to the earnings of the tenants. Need is king—that's the philosophy behind this housing. One of the differences between Milwaukee's veterans' housing project and the federally sponsored one is that the latter pays 10 per cent of its rent for local real estate taxes. However, where the city-owned venture is self-liquidating, the federal project pays its way only 20 per cent. The federal government picks up the 80 per cent deficit. What it amounts to is that those of us who pay taxes are helping the needy pay their rent. If we could figure out how to provide low cost housing either through private enterprise or municipal effort, the federal government would not be in the real estate business. It's really that simple.

But the mark of a civilization is how well the "haves" take care of the "have nots." If private urban renewal cannot meet the housing needs of low income groups, as it cannot, it should graciously step aside and let the government do it. Private enterprise has a right to complain only if it is willing to do the job itself, and do it more efficiently.

I spent my youth in the slums where the present federally sponsored Hillside Terrace Project in Milwaukee is located. The dilapidated buildings that were so familiar to me were plowed up and in their place garden and multiple story apartments now stand. The character of the neighborhood changed for the better. The low income tenants walked with more dignity. They became better citizens. Though private enterprise paid for this via income taxes, it received a tangible return in the form of a more wholesome city climate in which to transact its business. In an indirect way, is not this type of return as real and definite as money in the bank?

The elderly are a special group in the low income segment of our population. Their need is more poignant and visible because so many of them are so helpless. How their need was creatively met is illustrated by a federally sponsored project in Milwaukee known as Convent Hill. A blighted square block was razed and in the center was erected an attractive high building surrounded by landscaped walks and gardens. The building contains 120 one-bedroom apartments ranging in rent from $30 to $50 per month. Convent Hill offers special amenities catering to the special needs of the elderly. There are emergency bells for each apartment, an assembly hall, a lounge and kitchen to cater to tenants' birthdays, anniversaries, and special parties, a shuffleboard area, a horseshoe pit outdoors, and garden space for those who liked to putter outdoors. I talked to these poverty-scarred tenants. They showed more pride and gratitude for their little apartments than many I know who live in $75,000 homes.

Proof of the dire need of low income senior citizens for housing could be found in the 1,000 applications for the 120 apartments. Elderly people clamored for these modest apartments because they wanted to get away from the noise and congestion of rooming houses and apartments where no one paid any attention to them and where the rents were higher. Convent Hill attracted the elderly because in addition to shelter it offered a way of life. Congregate living for the elderly, especially when it is well programmed, and at a price they can afford, gives them a new lease on life. Their remaining years can offer a few golden moments instead of grey loneliness.

In the early part of 1964, I vacationed on St. Thomas Island, one of the American owned Virgin Islands. From my $50-a-day room in Bluebeard's Castle Resort I looked out upon a group of apartments facing the Caribbean which from my window looked like a luxury development. In fact, my wife said, "Next year let's take one of those apartments if we decide to stay longer than a few weeks."

The next day I walked down from the Bluebeard Castle, perched halfway up a hill, to look over the apartments. To my surprise, I found, first, they were not as expensive as they looked from a mile away, but more surprising, I discovered it was an urban renewal public housing project with rentals ranging from $9 to $50 a month. The people living in those apartments came out of hovels and shacks. There were about 500 units, and 1,500 children roamed the open green areas in the velvety, year 'round 75° climate freshened by the sea breezes. One does not have to be a sociologist to know that something good happens to a family when it is given a chance to live in decent surroundings. From what I learned, the tenants in the project were among the best behaved on the island.

Private urban renewal is not in a position to meet the needs of these people. Public urban renewal is the only answer for them and for hundreds of thousands in our American cities. It has been demonstrated that replacing slums with decent housing changes sorrow and misery to dignity and hope. If it does that, public housing surely has a place in urban renewal.

PRIVATE AND PUBLIC URBAN RENEWAL COOPERATING

In dealing with urban renewal we must recognize that there is nothing holy or unholy about private or public enterprise. The main consideration is how best to meet the needs of people. It was inevitable that private and public urban renewal should collide, and point accusing fingers at each other. Public enterprise can become overambitious and attempt to encroach into areas where private enterprise can do the job better. And private enterprise often has tried to block public enterprise from meeting people's needs even when private enterprise was unable to do so. These collisions made it apparent that a creative partnership between private enterprise and government was needed, a partnership where each played a role to complement the efforts of the other. This has been started in many cities and is beginning to work.

City and Federal government cooperate with private enterprise

To overcome several of the stumbling blocks that confront private enterprise in urban renewal, municipal and federal governments have combined to condemn certain slum areas, with the federal government absorbing two-thirds and the city government absorbing one-third of the loss between the cost of assembling the land and the sale price to the private developer. The Carl Sandburg Village in Chicago, consisting of 2,000 modern apartments and beautiful open green areas where formerly the stench of slums was in the air, is an example of what can happen when the government and private enterprise join hands.

In Milwaukee, the Lower Third Ward Redevelopment Project, consisting of about fifteen square blocks, is another example of public and private enterprise in partnership to renew a commercial area. In this case, all has not gone so well as in the Carl Sandburg Village. The land chosen for urban renewal was once swampy, and extensive piling is required if a sizeable building is to have suitable foundation.

I purchased a square block in this area to construct an office, hotel and apartment building complex. To my great consternation, a test boring disclosed that the land rested on 100 to 150 feet of muck. The city was not aware of this condition until the results of my test boring were examined. City authorities graciously returned my $27,000 down payment. Subsequently I learned that the owners of the Marine Plaza office building, only a few blocks from my lot, had spent $2,500,000 for piling. I mention this to caution others to look into the soil condition before spending a lot of time and money for plans.

Several years later the City of Milwaukee designated 25 acres near the heart of its downtown as an urban renewal area and chose the entrepreneurs who successfully built the Carl Sandburg Village to develop a $40,000,000 apartment complex. This could not have been put together without public and private enterprise working creatively together. The hearts of cities are being renewed all over America by efforts such as these, and what is equally important, government and private enterprise are learning to regard each other with mutual respect as they plan, work and achieve together.

City government cooperates with private enterprise

MARINE PLAZA

The city of Milwaukee has a "tax freeze" ordinance designed to encourage private redevelopment efforts. In effect, the ordinance defers a new appraisal—for as many as 30 years —of a building that replaces slum commercial structures. The area of redevelopment must embrace more than 100,000 square feet.

In 1960, the Marine National Exchange Bank decided to promote a new office building and parking structure, using the tax freeze. The city's businessmen were split on this issue. One group urged the tax freeze to spur the $20,000,000 office building, and the other vehemently opposed it on the basis that it was unfair competition to owners of other buildings who bore the full real estate tax load. For an entire year this issue was bitterly debated between men who believed in strict private enterprise with no subsidies, and those who were ready to modify their *laissez faire* philosophy for the sake of progress.

Office building owners were joined by competing bankers against granting a tax freeze. City Hall sided with the progress group, and a seven-year tax freeze worth about $3,000,000 in tax forgiveness was granted to the Polaris Corporation, the company which was organized to build the Marine Plaza office building.

Many of the older office buildings in the city lost tenants to the Marine Plaza. I lost 10,000 square feet—$40,000 a year income—to the new building. The businessmen of the city are still divided as to the fairness of the tax subsidy. Those who participated in the $20,000,000 project feel that without the subsidy it could never have been built. They say it gave Milwaukee's downtown a shot in the arm, provided work for hundreds, created new real estate wealth, and where visitors and Milwaukeeans used to look at two square blocks of dilapidated buildings, they now see a modern green skyscraper etched against a blue sky.

What do I think about the subsidy? I have been hurt financially but I still think that the good it created for the city more than compensated for the little hurts that owners of office buildings suffered. I can also understand why others would disagree with me. The philosophy of private enterprise has been bent quite a little here. It is not a black and white issue. It is very much in the grey area. I side with the subsidy philosophy only because it is the better of two bad alternatives. I don't like the alternative of stagnation.

This dilemma points up in bold relief the problem of private enterprise being constricted and pushed into an ever narrowing corner by high real estate taxes, high land cost, high interest rates and high cost of construction. It's becoming more serious every year. The problem of progress and subsidy versus stagnation and unfair competition is becoming very acute and it will require many creative, agonizing decisions before a solution is found.

SHOULD THIS HOTEL BE SUBSIDIZED?

Milwaukee doesn't have a large first-rate hotel. There are several new 200 room motor hotels but not a first class convention hostelry that could handle 1,000 delegates. The Schroeder is the largest hotel in Milwaukee with 700 rooms but it is almost forty years old.

A feasibility study by one of the leading hotel accounting firms in the country was made to determine whether a thousand room hotel could be made to pay in Milwaukee. The findings were that it could not unless there was a subsidy. A Milwaukee businessman assembled 160,000 square feet of blighted commercial property and applied for a 14 year tax freeze in line with the findings of the expert hotel accountants. The city was split in the middle again. Those wanting progress were pushing for its erection, and the hotel interests were shivering at the prospect of more empty rooms if this subsidy is granted. And they had good reason to shiver because the hotel occupany in Milwaukee now is about 60 per cent, and with this subsidized new hotel, many of the highly mortgaged inns might founder. The tug of war between progress and subsidy versus stagnation and unfair competition is reaching an acute stage. There are no easy answers. It is easy to plug for progress in theory but when a hotel owner's business is at stake it becomes a life-and-death business matter. Those who were for the Marine Plaza subsidy are taking another long look into the 14 year tax freeze request. How far should the subsidy extend? Can we progress only at the price of death to other businesses? We need new insights and new real estate techniques to give answers to these questions. The following story gives a partial answer.

WEST ALLIS INN

West Allis is a suburb of Milwaukee. With its 80,000 residents, it is the fourth largest city in Wisconsin. Its downtown area has not had a new building for thirty-five years. Industry, business and public officials formed a committee to promote downtown West Allis. They hired a coordinator to tell the West Allis story to real estate developers, and that's how I became involved in erecting a seven story building consisting of a ninety-six room motor hotel on the first five floors, and two stories of office space on top.

In my feasibility study I made several projections and drew several conclusions—all, however, predicated upon one important condition which I demanded from the City of West

Allis. It was this: West Allis was to condemn six old residences contiguous to my land, raze them, create 100 finished parking stalls, and lease them to me for 40 years at $3,000 a year. The City of West Allis had the authority of eminent domain to create parking for such purposes, and so my request was granted, and I proceeded to build.

West Allis spent about $100,000 to create the parking area. In a way, this was a subsidy, but I pointed out to the public officials that in three years they would have their money back from the $35,000-a-year real estate taxes, and continue to receive the $3,000-a-year parking rental which was about 3 per cent return on its $100,000 investment. However, the most important benefit to West Allis, I stressed, would be the positive psychological effect of the towering new building (all other downtown buildings were two story walk ups) that would trigger the remodeling of the old structures and the adding of new ones. The warmth with which industrial men, businessmen and public officials received my idea melted some of the problems and irritations which I encountered in rezoning and changing some of the archaic ordinances that hindered the project.

And now why did I get into this $1,500,000 building venture? My conclusion was that I was meeting a need. That is basic. And I concluded there was a need because of the existence of business generators—a basic requirement necessary for any project to be successful.

A 4,000-bed veterans' administration hospital is not more than a mile away—less than eight minutes by car from The West Allis Inn. The Allis-Chalmers Manufacturing Company plant—three blocks away—now finds sleeping accommodations for 30 or 40 visitors and trainees daily in hotels and motels several miles from the plant. The Wisconsin State Fair Park, which during August attracts about one million people, is five blocks away. With these three main business generators I felt that ninety-six rooms should do well in West Allis. My prediction was vindicated by the fact that a successful local hotel chain bought it and is doing extremely well with it.

My projection for the demand for office space, however, went awry. You would think that a city of 80,000 without one elevatored office building would gobble up 15,000 square feet of space at $4 a square foot. I was wrong. After a year of solicitation, in which I circularized each West Allis professional and businessman with letters and brochures, I was able to sign up only one lawyer for 400 square feet. The answer to my offer of modern, air conditioned, walnut paneled offices had this refrain: "I am comfortable where I am at a third the price so why should I move?" Prospective entrepreneurs planning office buildings in small towns, please take note!

Fortunately, I had had the foresight to put in connections for more bathrooms on those upper two floors. It had cost $7,000, but it was good insurance. I changed the upper two floors to thirty-four additional rooms.

This project made sense both for West Allis and me. It took creative effort on the part of both of us to develop a program that was both in the interests of the citizens of West Allis and gave me room to maneuver as an entrepreneur. The parking arrangement could be construed as a subsidy. But it enabled me to get parking through the city's power of eminent domain, and cut my cash outlay by $100,000. A variation of this plan could be used in many American cities.

HOW PRIVATE ENTERPRISE CAN COMPETE
WITH PUBLIC HOUSING

There is a provision in the 1964 Housing Bill under Title 221-D3 which offers an opportunity for private enterprise to build for low income tenants by providing FHA, 50 year financing at 3⅜ per cent. Charitable or non-profit organizations can build such housing and receive 100 per cent financing. A private entrepreneur can get 90 per cent financing, but may not get more than 6 per cent return on his 10 per cent of the investment (most of which can be earned through entrepreneurial fees), plus a fee for management.

Fifty year financing at 3⅜ per cent interest should enable private developers to charge only about two-thirds of existing private enterprise rentals. In other words, private enterprise can create housing for the needy through a creative partnership with the government and get the government out of public housing. The question is, will private enterprise accept this challenge from the government and meet the housing needs of our low income groups? It is true that there isn't much profit for private enterprise under 221-D3, but neither is there any chance of loss. The sure thing is that any private enterpriser who builds for the low income groups will make a creative contribution to the low income people who need his help. These people will demand public housing if private enterprise fails to meet their needs.

The government's offer of long amortization and low interest rate is especially applicable in building for the elderly. Churches, labor unions, and charitable organizations can do a magnificent job on the non-profit basis of Title 221-D3, and private enterprise can demonstrate its conviction in how much it believes in the superiority of private over public housing by rolling up its sleeves and joining in partnership with the government to meet the needs of those who otherwise might continue to flounder in city slums.

3.

Selling the Charm
of Old Buildings

Urban renewal is the real estate wave of the future. Where wholesale renewal is taking place, cities have had to come to grips with the troublesome problem of how much of the existing property to raze and what to preserve. In Milwaukee, a committee headed by an architect has been clamoring for the preservation of old and unique architecture in urban renewal areas because, as he put it: "We want to retain the character of our city. Let's not tear down buildings we would gape at with wonder when we go sightseeing abroad."

Aside from the aesthetic value of old buildings, there is an economic value as well. The cost of construction is high, and preserving buildings that have many years of remaining useful life can save America billions in real estate wealth. It behooves us not to squander that wealth.

The following real estate stories illustrate how to cash in on the charm of old buildings.

Prolonging the life of an old building nets $225,000

Nobody wanted it. A dozen prospective buyers looked at it and turned it down—and for very good reasons.

The Pereles Building was a mess, inside and out. In the Gay Nineties, its high-ceilinged dignity was the talk of the town. It had not aged gracefully. The old and haggard gray brick exterior cried for help. Loose bricks imperiled pedestrians. Over the brick clung the grime and dust of eight decades.

The interior was a depressing study in decrepitude. The dimly lit lobby was dingy and uninviting. Two ancient elevators dared you to take your life in your hands for a slow trip upward. Corridors were studded with protruding pipes left from the gaslight era.

The tenants? They were a family who lived in what once was the office of an attorney; several Bohemian artists who paid $20 a month for their bare studios; a man who repaired violins and offered bargains in used ones; a doctor who paid $50 a month for 3,000 uncleaned square feet of office space—and kept them that way; and several other miscellaneous souls. When—and if—they all paid their rent, the building's annual income was $10,000 for its 35,000 square feet of rental area.

Of this, taxes took $4,000, and heat $2,000. Add insurance and other miscellaneous costs, and the total annual expenses far outran the annual income. No wonder no one wanted it!

At first glance it looked hopeless. Why did I buy it?

It was located one block from the City Hall and one block from two of the largest banks in Milwaukee. The foundation of the building was sound. With an exterior facelifting and interior rejuvenation, it might attract new and better-paying tenants. Could new tenants be persuaded to move into a building with a tarnished reputation? I thought they could.

I bought the Pereles Building at the end of World War II for $65,000. I had little money then, but I scraped together $7,000 for a down payment. On the strength of my previous record with smaller but successful remodeling projects, I persuaded a savings and loan association to grant me a first mortgage of $58,000 on the condition that I spend a minimum of $25,000 for remodeling in the first two years.

Step by step, tenant by tenant, I began to upgrade my first downtown remodeling project I painted and tuck-pointed the exterior for $1,500. It was done in a tan and gray alternating pattern. From a distance it looked sparklingly new Even close up, it looked respectable.

The lobby remodeling was an adventure in extremes. A contractor bid $21,000 for a new marble and wood lobby. Obviously, this would have been financially suicidal. A friend of mine suggested that I investigate a new product—a hard asbestos material impregnated with a smooth wood-grain surface To introduce the product, the local manufacturer was willing to sell it to me for 10¢ a square foot. I hired a carpenter, and in one week he had covered everything that was old and dreary in the lobby with this walnut-grained material. It cost me $250. A slim-line fluorescent tube covered with an aluminum grill separated the old high ceiling from the new walls throughout the lobby This attractive lighting cost $100.

Using this type of low cost but attractive creative remodeling, I was able to fill the building with new tenants within a year and a half. I spent $35,000—but raised the rent from $10,000 to $54,000 a year. I borrowed the $35,000 on the strength of the higher income from new tenants.

Among my tenants now were reputable lawyers, doctors, insurance companies, finance agencies and a title insurance company.

Gone was the bedraggled exterior look. The dingy interior was no more. The dying building came to life. It became a beehive of activity, put to its highest and best use.

I may have taken too long in telling the story, but, as you will read in another chapter in this book, the Pereles Building not only brought me a profit beyond my wildest dreams, but provided the leverage to build the Bockl Building ten years later.

The Pereles Building finally died, but it had a happy ending. The Marshall & Ilsley Bank, a block away, was accumulating land for a parking lot. The Pereles Building occupied the last 60 by 120 parcel of the square block. I called the president and told him: "The Pereles Building is now more valuable to you than to me. Based on its present income it nets $25,000 a year. I'll sell it to you for $225,000."

Within a month the deal was closed—at $225,000.

A beautiful new drive-in bank now stands where the Pereles Building used to be, a story of the old giving way to the new. The old was profitably restored and put to its highest use, until a still better use came along.

The real estate axiom to note here is that the highest and best use is an ever changing thing.

Giving a new lease on life to a seventy-five year old "lady"

At the turn of the century, farmers hitched their horses alongside the Steinmeyer Building. It was a farmers' mart then, a sort of Gay Nineties supermarket. After the farmers sold their wares in the city, they would stop at the Steinmeyer Building to buy their groceries before returning to their farms.

The first floor of 12,000 square feet was used for displaying merchandise in the manner that the supermarkets do today, and the upper five floors were used for storage and an extensive coffee-grinding operation. When I went through the building the acrid smell of coffee still permeated the air even though the abandoned grinding machinery had been gathering dust for several decades.

When the building was offered for sale, only two floors were leased—the first floor to a furniture company, and the second to several printers. The upper four floors were vacant. The building was of mill construction but unusually well built. The red brick facade with its tall flagpole was a famous landmark in the city. It was located four blocks north of Milwaukee's 100 per cent downtown business district. Its neighbors were characterless, blighted buildings.

When the owners put the Steinmeyer on the market at $250,000 they thought it was a giveaway. They were in for a rude awakening. No one wanted it. And for a good reason. The rental from the first two floors was about $20,000 a year. The fixed expenses such as taxes, heat, insurance, and maintenance was about $15,000 a year. Why should anyone have been foolish enough to pay $250,000 for it?

After actively exposing the property on the market for a full year, the unpleasant fact that it was not worth more than half the asking price finally dawned on the owners. I bought it for $130,000.

The Steinmeyer had two strikes against it. It was in a rundown, congested area, and, because it was so close to down town, the tax assessor penalized the owner with an unrealistically high assessment.

I must have been more impressed with the building's ancient charms than were my prospective tenants. What I called "Gay Nineties atmosphere" they called old-fashioned blight. It was apparent that I wouldn't be able to make an enchantress of this 75 year old dowager by just powdering her face. She needed a new hair-do, and a face lifting as well.

I built a modern lobby using flush fluorescent lighting, a fissured acoustical tile ceiling, asphalt tile floor, and wood-paneled walls. It was in striking contrast to the old, but it gave it a needed new lift. I converted the old freight elevator into an automatic, self-operating passenger type. I steam cleaned the grimy red brick exterior. The new red color leaped out from the layers of dust. The building looked forty years younger.

Now I was ready to begin renting office space at one dollar per square foot per year. I knew I could not attract doctors and lawyers. Instead I directed my sales campaign toward printers, charitable agencies, artists, manufacturers' representatives, and the like.

The low price of a dollar per square foot and my concentrated campaign on selected low-paying groups of tenants paid off. I leased 5,000 square feet to a group of commercial artists who were captivated by the north light and the Gothic windows. The Wisconsin Heart Association needed lots of space but had little money in its budget for rent. Its officers admitted they were getting a bargain when they were charged only $600 a month for 7,000 square feet, partitioned into private offices, with tiled ceilings, asphalt tile floors and fluorescent lighting. A fur auction association needed 7,000 square feet at certain times of the year to show their mink pelts to customers, and could not afford to pay more than $500 a month for open space. We built it for them. They were delighted with it. I was even able to lease 2,000 square feet of space to an insurance company because it couldn't resist the low price.

Within a year I filled the building. The gross annual rent was $60,000. The net was $30,000. I spent $130,000 for remodeling. The building was now worth close to $300,000. The 75 year old "lady" was bustling with activity. She was living again. Though she was not as beautiful as when the farmers wooed her three quarters of a century ago, she was feeling important—and had a new lease on life.

One day I was talking to a man who said he liked my "new" Steinmeyer building, that he would be interested in buying it if I would be willing to take an old building he owned in

trade. I agreed. We exchanged buildings on the basis of $285,-
000 for my building and $65,000 for his. I subsequently resold
the $65,000 building for what I paid for it.

The buyer of the Steinmeyer building liked it so well he
built a modern apartment in it which he and his wife used
as a town house.

The Steinmeyer deal was not a howling financial success
story. After all my remodeling, leasing, and trading I only
made a profit of $25,000. But there were other benefits. The
community had one of its landmarks renewed for another 25
years, I increased the gross national product by $130,000, I
provided good low-priced office space for deserving tenants,
and my organization was interestingly occupied in creative
work.

Merchandising charm and good management quadruples value of a building

By every rule in the real estate book, the old Goldsmith
Building should have been relegated to the typical loft building having a rental value of fifty cents a square foot. The
only advantage it had over similar buildings was location. But
some other buildings equally well located did not do half so
well as the Goldsmith Building.

It was of mill construction. It still had its original oak floors.
Its distinguishing architectural mark was a 50 by 80 foot light
well that extended from the third floor to the skylight above
the eighth floor. Thus, these floors had an atrium arrangement, with the offices surrounding the light well.

The Goldsmith Building's 50,000 square feet of net rentable
area is yielding $200,000 a year, and has a value of about
$1,000,000. I have sold buildings of similar size and vintage,
but not as well located, for between $50,000 to $150,000.
What was the magic its owners used to make an old building,

which by the wildest stretch of the imagination could not
have been valued at more than $250,000, worth $1,000,000?

There was a combination of reasons. First, its youthful and
well informed property manager made the important decision
to convert the building into a medical center. This took courage because he turned away good commercial tenants in order
to establish the medical image he desired. But it paid off because eventually he filled it with the leading medical specialists
in the city. He was able to do it in spite of the fact that the
Goldsmith Building was landlocked and without close-in parking. But the manager gave them something more important
to make up for it. He gave them expert understanding of the
physician's needs.

A doctor is a special tenant. He is a perfectionist. His requirements must be met more fastidiously than those of any
commercial tenant. The manager of the Goldsmith Building
was a leader in the Building Owners and Managers Association, locally and nationally. He became a medical building specialist, and because of the specialized knowledge he acquired
in pleasing doctors, his building became the most prestigious
and sought-after medical address in Milwaukee. In addition
to his specialized medical building managerial skill he also
developed a friendly host-guest relationship with his meticulous tenants. Nor did he stop there. With a touch of the artist
he converted the building's physical minuses into charming
pluses.

The light well could have become old fashioned, dated
architecture, but with a few deft touches he created a French
Quarter feeling by painting the corrugated iron balusters white,
the six story high interior well in delicate shades of blue, gold
and yellow, lining the corridors with multi-colored plants in
multi-colored pots, and lighting the entire area with Italian
blown glass light fixtures from Venice.

Without creative management the Goldsmith Building would

have become just another decrepit economic liability. As long as the exclusive medical building image will be imaginatively shored up by unusual management, the Goldsmith Building will command a million dollar price. Its value, however, could topple to half in a few years if management slips and to one quarter, if it becomes shoddy. Too few investors are keenly enough aware of the close interdependence between management and value.

The Goldsmith Building is a prime example of how merchandising the charm of an old building can, with superb management, quadruple the value of investment real estate.

A lecturer's key word starts a chain reaction

Bresler Galleries was the mecca of art lovers for half a century. Some of the leading artists of our country showed their paintings there. Its picture frame department was nationally known. Its craftsmen framed many world famous paintings. Bresler Galleries was located on Milwaukee Street, the 100 per cent quality street of Milwaukee. In its heyday it occupied all three floors of the 80 by 100 foot Bresler Building, but as time went on, its business had dwindled to the point where it was occupying only one half of the first floor. It was paying $350 a month rent. The rest of the building was vacant.

The elderly owner wanted $120,000 for it, and of course, based on income, no one wanted it. My offer of $75,000 was quickly turned down. Unless I was ready to pay $120,000, the broker told me, the owner would not sell.

I was listening to a real estate appraisal lecturer one day when the following statement changed my thinking: "Each city has certain unique locations which cannot be duplicated in any other part of the city. These unusual locations in cities of as low as 50,000 population bring as much as $1,500 a front foot, because like diamonds, they are rare."

My mind quickly raced to the Bresler Building. Certainly that location was unique. I realized with a new sense of awareness why the 4,000 square foot quality women's apparel store to the north grossed three-quarters of a million dollars a year in sales. The next day I called the broker and offered $120,000. It was accepted. The lecturer, in effect, sold the building for the owner. The broker failed to use the secret word: "rarity." It was the dynamic selling point of his listing.

A quality men's apparel shop, I thought, would be the logical tenant for the Bresler Building. I talked with a broker who represented a leading men's clothing merchant. There was interest, but negotiations dragged along until I lost interest. In the meantime, the owner of Bresler Galleries, learning that the building was sold and that I was looking for tenants, became frantic. He knew his $350 monthly rental would be raised considerably. When I told him he would have to pay $750 a month for his forty foot store and the basement area where his frame department was located, he told me he would have to go out of business.

However, friends of art came to his rescue. A group of wealthy, art loving women formed a corporation and backed the Bresler Galleries with new capital. Their lawyer called me and said the new group joining with the owner were ready to sign a seven year lease at $750 a month. I accepted his proposal over the phone. The leases were being drawn, and they were to be signed on a Friday.

On Thursday, one day before the signing, the broker representing the quality men's clothing merchant, with whom I had been dealing earlier, came to my office and said his client would lease the entire building at $28,000 a year for fifteen years. It was an excellent deal for me. Based on the length of lease and the credit rating of the lessee I could mortgage the building and sell it with a sure $50,000 profit for me. As the broker was making the offer he noticed a peculiar expression on my face.

"What's the matter, George?" he asked. "You seem troubled. It's the deal you wanted, isn't it?"

"It certainly is, Bob, but the trouble is I can't accept it. I made a promise to Bresler to lease them their store."

It was the only decision I could make, but I must confess, it hurt. The only comfort I received for not accepting this profitable lease was Bob's remark, as he was leaving: "George, though it's costing me money, I admire your decision."

Bresler Galleries did not want to make any changes to their store. I thought it had a dilapidated look but what looked dilapidated to me must have looked artistic to them. I offered no objections.

The second floor had about 5,000 net rentable square feet. Half of it had a Florentine motif, with a clay tile floor, which one of the patrons of Bresler Galleries told me cost $20,000 to install. The window opening on Milwaukee Street had a small patio enclosed with black corrugated iron. The ceiling was in fresco plaster. I knew it would only appeal to art connoisseurs so I solicited several of the leading artist groups in the city, and was successful in signing a seven year lease with one of them. Their enthusiasm for the arty aesthetics of the space matched mine in getting them as tenants. It was a mutually happy deal.

Across the hall on the second floor was a space which I thought would lend itself for an exclusive beauty shop, catering to the elite. Before offering it I created a Gay Nineties atmosphere by carpeting the second floor stairway walkup, installing colonial light fixtures, and papering the walls with old plantation scenes to blend in with the old-south motif. I searched for the type of beauty operator who would blend in with the arty surroundings, and finally found a man and wife team who told me I offered them exactly what they had been looking for.

The third floor presented the most interesting problem. It consisted of an 80 by 100 foot clear-span ballroom with a twenty-two foot high ceiling. I was told by the seventy-five year old broker who sold me the building that in his youth at the turn of the century he frequented this stately dance hall in search of his romantic inclinations. Since there was no elevator in the building, leasing this space presented quite a challenge. My twelve year old daughter (who was taking dancing lessons) led me to the answer. When I called for her one afternoon at the dancing studio I noticed how dingy and cramped the quarters were. Here, I thought, was the answer to my quest for a ballroom tenant. Before I left I made an appointment with the dancing instructress to show her the third floor. When she saw it she couldn't stop raving about it. I leased it to her for $225 a month. She put her students to work painting walls and sanding floors. They made the studio gleam with brightness. Using pieces of antique furniture, knickknacks and arty doodads, she and her students created a terpsichorean atmosphere which they told me was superior to any they knew of in the Middle West.

I leased the remaining first floor store to a carpet company and I built the income from $350 a month to $28,000 a year. I did it with a remodeling expenditure of only $25,000. I preserved the old charm wherever it was feasible, cashing in on aesthetic economy whenever possible. For instance, the first floor entrance leading to the second floor had two 15 foot tall doors. My first reaction was to remove them and install a modern entrance. It would have been a case of poor judgment and poor economics. I hired a decorator who removed about twenty coats of old paint from the doors. By applying a gray-white shade of paint, he gave the doors an antique look, and the building a distinctive entrance that would have cost several thousand dollars. It cost me one hundred dollars.

With a $28,000 gross rental and an $18,000 net, I was able to sell the building for $180,000, giving me a profit of $35,000. This wasn't bad—only $15,000 shy of what I could have earned if I had taken the men's apparel shop deal!

But by preserving the old and adding the new only where necessary, I had breathed fresh economic life into a charming building. Indirectly, I had bolstered a worthwhile but dying art company, and had changed a dusty ballroom into one of the nation's fine dance studios.

Every city has its Sleeping Beauties—princesses from another era that await the kiss of imaginative ideas to awaken them to new life and new profits for investors.

4.

How to Get Into Big Deals with Little Money

Just as a "hungry" fighter, eager for victory, makes a good fighter, so does a "hungry" businessman, eager for success, make a good businessman. A "hungry" man with good ideas finds a way to put them to work. The danger is that the hungry fighter may become a dirty fighter, the hungry businessman may become a ruthless businessman and the hungry man with ideas can easily degenerate into an irresponsible promoter.

Getting into big deals with little money becomes a real estate science only when someone with creative ideas screens them carefully, looks thoughtfully into their feasibility, and puts forth his maximum effort to realize them. While the man with ideas is risking little of his own money, he is in effect risking a great deal—his reputation, all his future earnings. If his inordinate ambition to succeed carries him beyond a concern of what will happen to his backers, and he fails, he may be foreclosing forever his chances to put any of his good ideas to work. On the other hand, if he handles other people's money successfully, investors and mortgage companies will beat a path to his door. And when that happens, the man with ideas can become more selective and thereby increase their

71

success. I suppose this is what is meant by success begetting success.

The following are three examples of deals in which ideas, more than money, gave life to "white elephant" brick and mortar, and an example of a simple finance technique which got me into a million dollar deal without any money.

How I obtained control of a $500,000 building with no money down

An adventurer in real estate must be keenly aware of facts. Unusual facts often provide the key to unlocking a deal. Here is an example.

First, a profile of a building. It's on the northwest corner of North 7th Street and West Wisconsin Avenue, two blocks from Milwaukee's largest hotel. It is 125 by 150 feet. The east half of the building is mill construction and the west half concrete. It has 80,000 square feet of floor space. Years ago, most of the building was used by an automobile agency.

When I first investigated it, only four of the seven retail shops on the street floor were rented; half of the upper four floors were vacant. Most of the space above the first floor was occupied by printers. The vacant portions still showed oil slicks from automobiles parked there years earlier.

The profile of the owner is more pertinent. He was 72 years old, wealthy, and in a mood to sell. Weak management had held the rental down to $40,000 a year. The expenses were about the same, yet the owner wanted $500,000 for the building. He frankly admitted that his price was not justified on income, but stressed the vacancy for additional income, and the site's future potential. I was aware of this potential, but the $500,000 price was a mountainous obstacle.

"How do you intend to invest your money if you get your price?" I asked him.

"In mortgages," he answered. "Perhaps you'll help me find some good ones," he added with a twinkle in his eyes.

"Do you realize," I said, "that since you've probably depreciated your building to zero, your income tax on the $500,000 may well be over $100,000?"

"I see no way out of it," he said. "I've had Uncle Sam for a partner a long time."

My train of thought was taking on momentum.

"How would you like to sell your building, invest your money at the same time, and, as a sweetener, not to have to pay income taxes while doing it?"

"It sounds good. But what are you driving at?"

"Well," I said, "listen carefully. See if this doesn't make sense both for you and for me—and still satisfy Uncle Sam."

"All right, shoot! But it better be good because I'm pretty good at tearing schemes apart if they don't make sense, and when I can't tear one down I've got a pretty good lawyer who is even better at it than I."

"Here it is," I said. "You lease the building to me for fifty years on the basis of a $500,000 value capitalized at 4 per cent or $20,000 a year. This is $20,000 a year more than you are getting from your building at present, since your expenses are equal to your income. You pay income taxes only on the rental you receive every year. You pay no taxes on a sale— yet it is tantamount to a sale. What I am saying is this: you are in effect selling the building for $500,000 and simultaneously investing it with me at 4 per cent using your own building in which you have a lot of confidence as your collateral. Pricewise, returnwise, and taxwise it makes a lot of sense for you, doesn't it? But it would not be a good deal unless this plan also makes sense for me. It does, and I will tell you why.

"I believe that if I spend $75,000 to remodel your building and then rent the vacant space, I can bring the rent up to $80,000 a year. Thus, after $40,000 expenses and paying you the $20,000 yearly rental, there will be $20,000 left. That would be a very good return on a $75,000 remodeling investment."

"Would you guarantee to spend the $75,000 within, let's say, two years, as a condition to the deal?" the owner said with a spark of interest.

"I'd say it's fair," I said. I knew I could not bring the rental to $80,000 a year unless I spent at least $75,000.

I could see my plan take root. The more we talked the more convinced we became that it was a good deal for both of us.

We closed the transaction with no money exchanging hands, and I was in control of a $500,000 piece of good downtown real estate.

Using direct mail advertising, selective solicitation, and the help of other brokers, I obtained tenants on whose additional income I was able to borrow the money needed for remodeling. Actually, I spent $100,000, and got the rental up to $85,000 a year.

I subsequently sold my leasehold interest in the building to a man who used the $50,000 equity he had in an apartment building as a down payment, and assumed my $100,000 remodeling mortgage.

Within several months I sold the apartment building and paid the government taxes on a $50,000 profit.

Eight years later the purchaser of my leasehold sold it for $130,000. He had paid up the $100,000 remodeling mortgage out of profits. Thus, Uncle Sam received his taxes on the long term gain profit. The elderly fee owner has been receiving his yearly $20,000 payments, and Uncle Sam was getting his taxes from him as well.

So, you see, everyone gained. The fee owner is receiving $20,000 a year more than when the deal was made. For all practical purposes he sold the property, paid no taxes, and simultaneously invested the proceeds safely at 4 per cent. I earned $50,000. The man who owns it now clears $20,000 a year. He is a satisfied investor.

And what is equally important—a building got a new lease on life. It's bustling with activity. Its new tenants are enjoying good functional office space at little more than one dollar per square foot per year.

The city has gained, I have gained, and Uncle Sam has gained, and all the tenants and workers who have been touched by this deal have gained. You will do an owner of a similarly neglected building a favor if you discover him, and present a common sense plan that is mutually attractive.

Creative risks can be sold

The carpeting business was changing. Like many other downtown businesses it was caught up in the flight from blight to the more open spaces on the outskirts of the city. The 30,000 square foot, three-story Morley-Murphy Building was landlocked in an area several blocks south of the heart of Milwaukee's downtown. Its owners saw the handwriting on the wall. It was too costly to buy a building next door to provide ample parking. The cost of material handling in the multiple-story building was too high. They sensed a reluctance on the part of their customers to shop in the parking-starved, congested downtown area.

The Morley-Murphy owners decided to move, and put their building on the market. They started with a $200,000 asking price, came down to $150,000, and when I had gotten wind of the fact that the State Soil Conservation Department was looking for larger quarters, I took a chance and offered $105,000 for the building—$100,000 to the owners, and $5,000 to the broker. With what must have been a sigh of relief, the owners accepted.

My hunch about the State Soil Conservation Department proved right. They were cramped in 15,000 square feet. The 30,000 square foot Morley-Murphy Building was ideal for them. The estimates of remodeling costs to meet the Soil Conservation's needs came to $25,000. I agreed to lease the premises for $22,500 a year for five years, the lessor to pay the real estate taxes and the lessee to pay for the heat.

Before my deal with the Morley-Murphy owners was closed, but with a letter of intent for a five year lease in my hand, I offered this package deal to an investor for $155,000. I told him I paid $105,000 for the building, that the cost of remodeling would be $25,000, and that I wanted a $25,000 profit for the risk and assembling the deal. I made the point that since the real estate taxes and insurance were about $3,500 a year, his yearly return would be $22,500 less $3,500, or a net of $19,000 for a $155,000 investment. That came to about a 12 per cent return.

My prospect liked the rate of return, but he didn't like my making $25,000 on the deal.

"Charlie," I said, "you know this is a good investment for you. Why don't you keep your eye on what you're getting rather than on what I'm making? Remember, I could have had this building vacant for several years and lost money. Why don't you be glad that I'm making $25,000, and I'll be happy that you're getting a 12 per cent return. And to sweeten the deal, Charlie, I can get you a $115,000 mortgage if you want it."

"O. K., you win," he said resignedly.

The deal was closed, Morley-Murphy moved to the outskirts, the Soil Conservation Department moved in, Charlie made an excellent investment, and I earned $25,000 by taking a calculated risk—an important ingredient in real estate adventuring. Risking creatively can often be substituted for money —in fact, a well thought out risk is more valuable in a deal than money unimaginatively used.

Ideas that kept a building alive

In 1948 a successful candy salesman decided to get into the real estate business. He bought a 120,000 square foot, six story wholesale grocery warehouse and began looking for tenants. They were available but somehow he wasn't able to sign them up. Perhaps it required a different type of skill from selling candy. At any rate, a year passed and his building remained vacant.

One evening I attended a lecture on the advantages of a 99 year lease. The next day I met the candy salesman and said: "I learned something about a 99 year lease last night that could make sense for you and me. I know you're one of the great candy salesmen in America, but selling space is something else. Why don't you stick to selling candy and leave the leasing to me? What I'm trying to say is that you lease your property to me for 99 years and get a steady income, instead of bucking a vacant building. That's for me, not for you."

Several days later we met and agreed on the following terms:

I was to form a shell corporation which was to sign a 99 year lease on the basis of $28,000 a year for the first fifteen years, $20,000 a year for the next ten years, and $15,000 a year for the remaining 74 years of the lease. I agreed to have the new corporation pay two years rent in advance.

Tucked away in a corner of my mind was the knowledge that the Army Reserve Training Center was looking for space near the downtown area. I struck a spark of interest. I pointed out the advantages of my space and the low price to the top army brass of the procurement division. I got a favorable reaction all the way from the captains to the colonels. But it wasn't enough. I didn't get final approval until I received the nod from a brigadier general who flew in from Washington. We signed a lease for 60,000 square feet at $35,000 a year for five years.

On the strength of the lease, I induced my bank to loan me the $56,000 two year advance rental called for in the 99 year lease. I simply paid the first two year rent to the bank instead of to the lessor.

Within sixty days after I signed up the army, I leased the balance of the space to a plastic manufacturing company for $35,000 a year. After deducting my leasehold rent and fixed expenses, I was left with a net profit of $25,000 a year. This overage was used toward a $125,000 remodeling loan to install new plumbing, heating, electrical wiring, fixturing, and new partitioning.

After five years the army moved to a training center of its own, and by coincidence the plastic firm which used the balance of the space went bankrupt at the same time. I had a vacant building, no money in the corporation, and no debts—I had amortized the $125,000 remodeling loan from the profits of the last five years.

When the army and the plastic company moved in, and I was showing a $25,000 yearly net return, my landlord candy salesman offered $125,000 profit for my leasehold rights. When I called him after I lost my tenants, and asked what he would offer for my stock now, his answer was quick, and to the point, "Nothing!"

I presume what he had in mind was that if I couldn't rent the building I would turn it back to him with the $125,000 improvements I put into it. And I would have done it had it not been for a tip I received that the General Merchandise Co. was bursting with expansion activity, and that they might be in the market for a building like mine. I called the president and told him he was in a position to get a tremendous space bargain if he could act within sixty days. The owner of the firm was the kind of a man who intuitively "smelled" a bargain before he saw it. After I showed him the building and explained the terms he said, "George, I'll take it."

He signed a ten year lease on the basis of cutting the $25,000 profit I was getting before I lost my tenants to $10,000 a year net to me. He offered it out of a combination of reasons. The building suited his needs, he liked the idea that I disclosed the terms of my prime lease, and being a businessman who was profit oriented, he was too gallant to squeeze all the profit out of my deal. He could have, if he had wanted to.

By the time the General Merchandise Co. installed its material handling equipment, modernized the two elevators, improved the dock area, and changed partitions to suit its needs, it had spent $125,000 on the building. The value of my leasehold went right up, from nothing to $100,000, as soon as I signed the lease. This is a dramatic illustration of how the value of a building can fluctuate, and how difficult it is to arrive at a valuation except through the income approach.

The story does not end here. Seven years later, the General Merchandise Co. grew so big that it vacated 400,000 square feet of several multiple-story buildings it was leasing in the downtown area, including mine, and built a plant of its own on the outskirts of Milwaukee, a typical instance of flight from downtown blight. I was left with a vacant building again. Of course, the General Merchandise Co. remained liable for the remaining three years of the lease at the rate of approximately $55,000 a year—this amount being the sum of my $10,000 profit, $28,000 leasehold rent, and the remaining fixed expenses such as real estate taxes, heat, etc.

General Merchandise Company's attempts to sublet the space it was not using were unsuccessful. One day an idea

struck me. While it was still hot in my mind I called the
president of the company and said: "Dave, you've got almost
three years left on your lease at about $55,000 a year, or a
liability of $165,000. What would you think of this proposi-
tion? Give me $80,000 in cash and I'll release you from your
lease. I think it's a mutually fair deal. I get paid for taking a
risk, and you cut your liability in half.

"It makes sense, George. Let me take it up with my board,
and you'll hear from me within the week."

I got the $80,000, and for the third time I was confronted
with the same vacant building. This was in 1961 when finding
tenants for multiple story buildings was far more difficult than
in 1948, when I leased it to the army and a plastic firm, and
in 1953 when I was bailed out by the General Merchandise
Company. In 1961 the flight from downtown to the outskirts
became an exodus. Dozens of buildings like mine were vacant.
However, I enjoyed two advantages. One was that my building was of steel and concrete, while most of the others were
mill constructed. The other was the $80,000 cash in my cor-
poration which gave me several years of staying power.

Two unrelated things happened which enabled me to lease
the building for the third time. They started with a spur of
the moment idea, and led to two long-term leases. I had occasion to pick up a sundry item at a wholesale medical supply
company, and noticed that the firm was operating on six
floors of a 20 foot wide building that had no parking and
poor loading facilities. I asked to see the president of the company. It was my good fortune to find him in.

"You're operating in awfully narrow and vertical quarters,"
I said. "Shouldn't you be on one floor?"

"I sure should," he said. "But I own the building and I'm
stuck with it. No one will buy it."

"You've just sold it," I said seriously.

"To whom?" he asked.

"To me. There's only one catch," I said. "I'll buy it providing you become a tenant of mine in a building I control several blocks away."

"I hope you're not kidding," he said, "because I'm interested."

Within several months I signed a lease for two floors of my building with the Roemer-Karrer Medical Supply Co. at $18,000 a year for ten years. I paid $50,000 for its 10,000 square foot narrow building. I resold it two years later at a $20,000 loss, but it was profitable to take the loss in order to gain a tenant.

While attending a board meeting of a Red Feather Agency, dealing with rehabilitating retarded people through work therapy, I heard complaints from the director of the agency that their space was too cramped, cut up into too many parts of the building, and generally inadequate. After the meeting, I suggested to the director that he look at my building.

"But our budget is low and our demands are high," he replied. "We can only pay 50 cents a square foot heated. We need many amenities catering to the infirm, and we have no money with which to provide them."

"There's no harm in looking," I said.

"Certainly not," he replied.

The director liked my building but he warned me again that it would take a lot of money to get them into it. But with the $80,000 in the corporation, I felt that I couldn't find a more worthy tenant to spend it on. I leased four floors consisting of 64,000 square feet to the rehabilitation agency for $32,000 a year. The director's warning was not in vain. I spent all of the $80,000 getting them in. It was a bad real estate deal but for a good cause. Several months later I leased the remaining 16,000 square feet of basement area for $6,600 a year to bring my total annual rent to $56,600. By this time my leasehold rent dropped from $28,000 to $20,000 a year, and my yearly net return came to approximately $17,000.

By this time both the building and I were getting tired. I sold my leasehold interest for $100,000.

Old multiple story buildings are becoming more and more difficult to rent. No money is needed to acquire them—only ideas. Unfortunately there are many more of these buildings than there are entrepreneurs with creative ideas.

A finance idea gets me into a million dollar deal without a cent of my own

In 1953, a beer bottle manufacturer ingeniously put together a real estate deal which would have been a credit to any professional realtor.

The Delta Manufacturing Company decided to move its operations from Milwaukee, and put its 200,000 square foot building on the market. Nine acres of land, in the heart of an industrial area, went with it. The beer bottle executive got the ear of one of the nation's leading brewers, and received a promise from him that he would lease the building for seventeen years. With the backing of the lease he bought the building for a million dollars and arranged for a million-dollar loan payable in seventeen years at 4¼ per cent interest. The terms of the 100 per cent mortgage provided that the lease be pledged as security, and that all rents be applied to the loan until paid.

It was a good deal for the Delta Manufacturing Company because the company received close to the asking price; it was a good deal for the brewer because the building was ideally suited for his needs; it was a good deal for the mortgage company because its risk was secured by a lease from one of the wealthiest brewers in the country; and it was a good deal for the beer bottle executive because he acquired a million dollar building without any money.

Six years later I came into the picture. In the course of a conversation with a friend of mine, he described the Delta deal to me, and concluded with this remark:

"It's a fantastic deal A. D. got himself into. But it has a weakness. He has to pay income taxes on earnings which he won't realize until he either sells the building or owns it free and clear eleven years from now. Accelerated depreciation has caught up with him."

I knew the beer bottle manufacturer. He was a wheeler and dealer who always needed money for new projects. He was in a high income bracket. Paying income taxes on money he wasn't getting, I surmised, was not to his liking.

I got A. D. on the phone and said, "A. D., how would you like to get a quarter of a million dollars in cash and stop paying income taxes on $25,000 a year you aren't getting?"

"Georgie," he said, "I'd love it. How do I do it?"

"Sell me your Delta Building for a million dollars—what you paid for it—subject to your present $750,000 mortgage. That's how you can do it."

"You're talking about my safest trouble free investment."

"But it's not doing you any good, and you know it."

It's necessary to explain here that A. D. was a man of about 55 who had no children. I knew he was more interested with what he could do with money now rather than wait for its accumulation eleven years from now.

"Well, it's a good enough idea for me to invest a lunch in you," A. D. said. "How about tomorrow?"

He couldn't resist my twin argument of getting a quarter of a million dollars in cash and the tax saving on about $25,000 income which he was earning through his mortgage amortization. We made the deal.

Though my position was not as good as when A. D. got into

the deal, I, nevertheless, tried to get as close to it as possible. I did it this way:

I borrowed the entire $250,000 equity needed for the deal from a bank and assigned my interest in the brewer's lease. I pointed out to the loaning officer that in eleven years the building would be free and clear, and he would have a prime lien on a million dollar building. His only risk, I suggested, was whether the lessee would continue to pay the rent. And, of course, that was not a great risk because the brewer was worth more than the bank! I got my $250,000 loan, and by upping my depreciation base back to a million dollars plus the interest deduction on the $250,000 loan, I actually showed a loss for the first several years.

At the termination of the seventeen year lease the brewer has an option to buy the building for $750,000 in cash, or extend the lease for another two five-year periods at $50,000 a year net to me. In either case, the bank's $250,000 unamortized loan will be safe. Though no money was invested in the deal, every financial move was conservative, and made sense to all parties concerned. Even the United States government, which was held off from getting its taxes because of increased depreciation and interest deduction, will eventually have its day when the building is sold. It already received a good chunk of it when A. D. sold the building and paid a tax on $250,000 profit.

I believe there is nothing wrong in being able to get into a big deal without money if the financial techniques are grounded in sound economics. There are many deals like this in every city. A broker or an entrepreneur can breath life into a set of facts and circumstances, and create deals where none seem to exist. All it takes is sincerity and originality. By understanding facts, giving them a fresh arrangement, and communicating them with logical lucidity, a tycoon preoccupied with his own affairs can be perked up to respond to a revolutionary real estate deal. The professional real estate entrepreneur should be the catalyst to convert old real estate situations into new ones. The Delta deal illustrates how easily it can be done.

5.

Creative Ideas That Sold
$200,000,000 of Real Estate

In a twenty year period our sales organization developed techniques which sold 15,000 parcels of real estate involving two hundred million dollars. These transactions were equivalent to selling every home, industrial building, store building, and office building in a typical United States city of 75,000 people. It has been tedious, painstaking and rewarding work.

What are the practical steps in starting a real estate organization? What are the insights and policies necessary to keep it expanding once it is successfully launched? If I had to limit my answers to two words they would be *sincerity* and *originality*. More effective than sales syllabuses and selling systems is genuine awareness of people's needs and the courage to do the unusual. Idealism must be linked to practical considerations. They go hand in hand. Each becomes weaker without the other.

Ideas that got me started

The custom in our city when I started in the real estate business was for brokers to take six month listings. In tying up properties for long periods of time the brokers did not feel strong obligations to get quick results nor did the sellers expect them. There was a mutual understanding that it took a long time to sell a house, and by custom the listing period of six months became the acceptable norm.

THIRTY-DAY LISTINGS

I decided that the quickest way to shatter one of the old real estate traditions was to advertise, "We have good reason to believe we can sell your property in 30 days." Sellers responded by asking about the idea. I explained that in taking a thirty-day listing I was willing to concentrate all of the advertising in thirty days instead of spreading it out over six months. I pointed out that by shortening the time and concentrating the advertising I could generate a great deal more interest in a property by putting it actively on the market than could be done by letting it remain passively for sale. It worked!

I was careful not to take listings which were over-priced. When I signed a thirty-day priced-right listing in a good location, I gave it the "gun"—I advertised it on Sundays and week days. The response was heartwarming. The psychological effect of prospects seeing other prospects going through the house at the same time sparked added interest. It wasn't unusual for me to show a typical good listing to as many as twenty prospects in a single week. In eight cases out of ten I would get a deposit close to the asking price within thirty days.

In the Real Estate Wanted column of the Milwaukee Journal I had a weekly ad stating in bold type the addresses of homes I sold in three days, ten days, eighteen days, and sometimes, when I was extremely lucky, in one day. This type of on-target advertising brought a flood of inquiries. Prospective sellers liked the idea of knowing whether they could have their house sold within one month. If it did not sell they were free to go to another broker, or renew for another thirty days. Since eight out of ten listings sold, the news about our results spread like wildfire. Within a half year I hired two salesmen to help with the increasing volume of business.

SECOND MORTGAGE FINANCING

I started my real estate business during the conventional mortgage days when there was no FHA, GI, or VA financing. A 65 per cent mortgage was a maximum loan in those days. I soon became aware that I could sell many more properties if I could arrange small down payment financing. People with good jobs were eager to buy homes, but couldn't, because they had only several hundred dollars for a down payment. I knew if I could figure out a way to sell homes with low down payments I could quadruple my business. I developed this plan:

When a home would not sell conventionally with 35 per cent down, we offered to buy the home from the owner for cash, disclosing to him our plan of mortgaging it ourselves, selling it with a small down payment, and taking our equity in a land contract or second mortgage. We offered this plan to the seller if he chose to sell with a small down payment. If he wanted only a cash deal, we then financed it in the following manner:

Let's say that we listed a property for $11,000 and couldn't sell it conventionally with a 35 per cent down payment. We would then offer the owner $10,000 in cash allowing a $500 commission for selling the property to ourselves and an extra $500 for the risk of guaranteeing the cash to the owner. We would sign an $8,000 mortgage with a savings and loan association and pay the balance of $2,000 in cash. We made our mortgage on the basis of the potential selling price of the real estate rather than on what we paid for it. We then advertised the property for $11,500 and sold it with $500 down, taking a $3,000 land contract or second mortgage subject to our first mortgage of $8,000. Since we did not have the cash to do this on a large scale, we would sell the $3,000 second mortgage or land contract equity at 25 per cent discount and get our $2,250 in cash. This added to the $500 down payment we received in cash, gave us $2,750 against the $2,000 in cash we had to invest to make up the difference between the $8,000 mortgage and the $10,000 purchase price. Thus we made a cash profit of $750 on this rather complex transaction.

This type of financing started a deluge of sales. I quickly added three more men. But manpower wasn't enough. I had to develop money sources to keep discounting my second mortgages and land contracts. Soon we were selling $500,000 worth of second mortgage "paper" a year, and buyers with good jobs were purchasing property through us with as low as $100 down.

We made everyone happy. The savings and loan associations made safe conventional 65 per cent mortgages, the buyers of the second mortgages and land contracts were making a good profit for taking strong risks, buyers were purchasing property which they otherwise could not buy, and we were averaging about 7 per cent cash commission on sales after taking each property through the second mortgage or land contract route. Though some of the people who bought homes in those days may have overpaid 5 to 15 per cent, had we not arranged to sell these homes with low down payments, they would not be owning them free and clear today. Small down payment home buying was the wave of the future and we recognized it, and put it to work, ten years before it became generally accepted through FHA and VA financing. We sold millions of dollars worth of homes with the aid of secondary financing. Now that homes can be bought with little down through private as well as publicly insured financing, second mortgage and land contract financing are no longer needed. However, it was an effective idea which helped give impetus to the high percentage mortgaging techniques available to the American home buyer today. The second mortgage idea is antiquated today but it helped us get started twenty years ago when it was new.

"HORIZONTAL CONDOMINIUMS"

The thirty day listing idea and the second mortgage financing technique gave our organization a selling momentum that was a pleasant surprise to me, but not quite so pleasant to my competitors. We had seven hustling salesmen who kept proving to the public that a shorter listing period, coupled with progressive mortgaging methods, brought results.

One creative idea leads to another. When the mind becomes alive it continues to probe for the new, the different, the unknown. Two successful ideas led to a third, and it was so good that it grossed $500,000 in commissions.

It started this way. A deal was put on my desk which involved six properties on one lot. Each of the four-room cottages had a frame basement and outside plumbing. They were located on a 60 by 150 foot lot with three cottages on one side of the 30 foot frontage, and three cottages on the other 30 foot frontage. The monthly rent averaged $15 per cottage. They had been sold and resold as a group several times, with each new buyer milking the investment more than his predecessors. By the time the property was presented to me, the cottages were in a dilapidated mess.

I purchased them for $2,500. My purpose was not to buy them as an investment, but to try out an idea that came to me while I was inspecting them. It was this: I would advertise each of the cottages for a thousand dollars with $100 down, and payments of $15 per month on the $1,400 balance to include interest and principal. To my pleasant surprise I sold all six of them within several weeks. I hired a good attorney to divide the 60 by 150 foot lot into six separate legally described parcels, reciting in each deed the rights that each had to common walks, sewers, water mains, and so forth.

The economics of the deal made sense. Our company signed a $1,700 first mortgage on the six cottages, and with the $600 we collected in down payments, we had only a $200 investment in the deal. Our land contract equity in the six cottages was six times $1,400 less $1,700 or $6,700. Not bad for a $200 investment! Then something happened which improved the deal still more. I noticed as I drove by the cottages several months later that two of the owners were putting in cement block basements. When I stopped to examine my "horizontal condominium" more closely, I found some improvements taking place in each of the cottages. In addition to the cement block basements other owners were installing plumbing, putting in flooring, and doing extensive wallpapering. They were doing the work themselves, or teaming up with their neighbors to help each other. Within a year the slum look gave way to a neat, pleasant environment. The new owners had more at stake and more pride of ownership than the previous milking investors.

Having successfully merchandised the six cottage "condominium," we launched an extensive program to buy properties with two or more parcels on one lot. Intuitively I felt we had a tremendous idea. I was right. Owners who were not doing too well with this type of property as an investment were glad to sell them to us. In one instance, we bought thirteen properties on one lot with one legal description. We sold it to thirteen owners. It was good for the new buyers, it made sense to the owner who was beginning to have trouble milking it, and, of course, we found it profitable to subdivide it. We bought and sold hundreds of such properties. Invariably, the new buyers would follow the same pattern of the six cottage owners. Though their homes were located on split lots, they would improve them, usually with their own labor, and brighten up their neighborhood.

Hundreds of tenants became property owners through our subdividing of these "horizontal condominiums." Though it created some problems, they were no more involved than the problems experienced in today's high rise condominium, which is now a legally accepted form of real estate ownership. While we were capitalizing on the "horizontal condominium" selling technique, we were subjected to some criticism by our competitors—perhaps because it was never done before. However, I am heartened by the fact that had it not been for our "splitting properties," hundreds of tenants would not have become home owners—and a home owner is usually a more responsible citizen than a tenant.

At first there was some problem in mortgaging the subdivided parcels, but when we explained the advantages of split ownership to the savings and loan associations, they were quick to see it our way. Hundreds of good mortgages were placed because of our new idea of subdividing "cluster" properties.

The "horizontal condominium" idea gave our organization another spurt in growth. Twelve busy salesmen were now covering the city for our firm. We were averaging twenty sales a month. Business was booming. Our original ideas were paying off. The old entrenched real estate firms were sniping at our innovations. But we were heartened by the fact that soon some of them began to copy our methods. We were converting critics into competitors. Our organization had the ball and we were running with it. In ten years we became one of the five leading real estate organizations in the city.

TRADING—A VEHICLE FOR SELLING

With thirty-day listing, second mortgage financing and horizontal condominiums we didn't have to discover the next new idea—we backed into it. We were turning away potential home buyers because many good prospects would tell us, "If we knew how much we could get for our home, we would be willing to buy yours."

This made us aware of trading as a means of selling homes. But being aware of an idea is one thing—crystallizing it and giving it visibility is another. This is how we developed the trading technique which skyrocketed our sales by the millions and commissions by the hundreds of thousands. Our newspaper campaign stressed this theme:

"For years you've been trading your car, now you can trade your home just as easily. You can sell your home and buy another in one operation. On the same day that you buy the home you want, you know how much you'll get for the one you own. It's that simple."

After several months we varied our campaign in this way: "Is your home too large, too small? Do you want to leave your present neighborhood for a better one? Are your monthly payments too high? We can help you by trading the home which no longer serves your needs for one that does." We would then give a list of addresses of homes we had successfully traded. The response was beyond our most optimistic expectations.

This is how we traded. We would accept an offer on one of our listings, and agree at the same time to buy the purchaser's home at an agreed-upon price. We would immediately begin advertising his home for sale. If we sold it before the first purchaser's closing date, we would close both deals simultaneously. This, of course, was the ideal situation. However, if we failed to sell the home we purchased, our company would sign a mortgage with a savings and loan association and pay the difference in cash so that the buyer we traded with had his money available to close his deal. Often the home we bought would not sell directly but would be involved in still another trade, and in several instances, we had a chain involving as many as five succeeding trades.

We increased our sales force to fifteen men because the

trading idea caught on like wildfire. Forty per cent of our sales were being made via the trade route. At times our office would have five trade chains going on at the same time. Trading as a means of selling homes is practiced in many parts of the country today but fifteen years ago we pioneered it in Milwaukee.

I soon realized that only a few of my salesmen really understood the art of trading. Those who did not possess a mathematical sense wanted no part of it. They were interested only in straight selling. Those who had a knack for figures and were able to communicate them clearly concentrated all their attention to trading. Several became experts. They were able to "see" deals which didn't seem to exist to direct selling salesmen. They were able to extract commissions out of complex situations because they knew how to make the turns on the circuitous trading route.

In the course of trading, we may use bad judgment occasionally and get stuck with "dogs." I remember at one time we accumulated an assortment of "odd lot" properties. I happened to know a certain broker who was trading a bit too wildly and got stuck with a number of "dead cat" properties.

One day I walked over to his office and said, "Walter, how would you like to trade your 'cats' for my 'dogs'? I have a hunch that my salesmen have become stale on my 'dogs,' and your salesmen have lost their zest dealing with your 'cats.' Let's trade."

After several days of sparring, negotiating, wheeling and dealing, we made the exchange.

My hunch was right. In a few months his salesmen got rid of my "dogs" and my salesmen got rid of his "cats." It was good old fashioned horse trading, and it worked.

Because a seventh of our population for one reason or another moves every year, trading as a means of selling real estate is here to stay. No modern brokerage office can afford not to have a trading department. The days when people live in the same home for several generations are gone. More and more people regard a home with not much more permanency than they do a car. And as new families are forming, growing larger, getting into middle age, and growing old, requirements for homes keep changing. And because neighborhoods change more rapidly than they did in the past, and job opportunities become more fluid as new communities open up, an increasing number of people will want to exchange their homes for others. No residential brokerage firm can be abreast of the new selling techniques unless it is abreast of the latest trading approaches.

Ideas that eased me into maturity

There is a time to run and a time to reflect. While I was getting started, I was running. Know-how and results were more important to me than acquiring wisdom. But it is unwise to keep running without pausing for wisdom to catch up. Fortunately, I did pause long enough to reflect on my running. Doing this started me on the road to responsible maturity.

Not to be ready for the point of change—from running to maturity—is running without direction, selling energies and talents at too low a price. If we settle for success unframed in idealism, we don't give our life's purpose the dignity it deserves. We lose much, and unfortunately in our hurry we don't fully perceive the magnitude of our loss.

PROVIDING FOR SALESMEN

The more successful salesmen become, the more recognition they seek. They want to become part of the enterprise they are building. Not to recognize this is to turn one's back on their yearnings and loyalties.

To consolidate our quick rise to real estate prominence, I sold 45 per cent of the common stock of my company at book value to several key men in my organization. This did as much to knit my business together as the new ideas which got me started. Without these top men our momentum would have lost its thrust. With them, we surged forward.

Important as it is to care for the key men, it is equally necessary to care for the sales staff as well. They want security and a place in the sun, too. And since there are many more $6,000 a year bread and butter salesmen than the exceptional $20,000 a year kind, it is important to plan for their future. A large organization cannot long prevail unless as much attention is given to the Indians as to the Chiefs.

To provide for the average salesman we instituted a profit sharing plan in which all salesmen participated. Our firm makes all the contributions from its earnings into a profit sharing plan, and distributes the proceeds according to a formula involving a salesman's leaving the company voluntarily, his death, or his retirement. In addition to offering stock ownership to the key men and profit sharing to all men, we provided a life insurance and health and accident program— with two-thirds of the cost paid by the company and one-third by salesmen and stenographic personnel. The latter programs have been used by several of our employees, and the monetary help available in their time of need gave me a rewarding feeling that we had helped alleviate some painful problems.

These sound, mature business decisions were responsible for my being able to build a forty man sales organization. The average salesman has been with me for 12 years. This mutual reliance is good both for the organization and the men. Unless the salesmen feel it in their bones that the organization is behind them, the organization has no right to expect them to be behind it.

Beyond stock ownership, profit sharing, and insurance protection, there are times when men need additional help. Sometimes a timely bit of financial aid can be the cement to keep a family from breaking up. Salesmen may run into periods of bad luck, or personal problems which curtail their income. An understanding firm must be ready to extend financial help, and see them through these "dry" periods. We have charged off about $25,000 in helping men through trying times. We feel that such losses are as much a fixed business expense as telephone, advertising or rent. Some of the men we have helped came out of their slumps, and became better men. We both gained. Real estate would indeed be a harsh business if it involved only making a profit. In the process of making a profit, we can help build men and make our business more ennobling.

REAL ESTATE SOCIOLOGY

It is one thing to read about civil rights, it is another to be on the battle line where the bullets are flying. Because we directed our energies toward volume sales, we became involved with the masses instead of the classes. We became the Sears-Roebuck brokers of the lower income groups. We rarely dealt with silk stocking prospects. This inevitably brought us face to face with the housing needs of the Negro in our community.

From 1950 to 1960 the Negro population of Milwaukee doubled from 30,000 to 60,000. Most of the Negroes settled in the city's core area of poor housing and low rents. As in many other northern cities, the Negro in Milwaukee wanted to break out of his ghetto, but the whites did not make it easy for him to do it. As the Negro moved into white neighborhoods there were complaints and accusations.

As brokers we took a neutral position, and objectively served the owners who wanted us to sell their properties. When they instructed us that they were unwilling to sell their properties to Negroes, and when Negro prospects called, we frankly told them of the sellers' wishes. With few exceptions the Negroes did not insist on buying such properties. But many sellers put no restrictions on their sales, and we sold dozens of properties in previously all-white areas to Negro families.

Initially, we found, the arrival of a Negro family in a white neighborhood set off a wave of turbulence, but the disturbances and fears would abate as the ratio of Negroes to whites increased. Then an orderly process of transition would begin.

The Negroes kept fanning out into white neighborhoods as more and more white owners agreed to sell to them. With the colored population doubling in ten years, they had to move somewhere. Our firm was responsible for the relocation of about 600 Negro families into new areas. We were subjected to the usual complaints. We were called various names, of which "block busters" was the kindest. But empty accusations don't hurt. We saw a business opportunity in serving the needs of people, and we set out to serve that need in the best way we knew. We take pride in having played a vital role in an orderly movement of a minority people from one neighborhood to another.

When we were getting started in the real estate business, savings and loan associations were unwilling to make mortgages to Negro home buyers. I went to a Catholic friend of mine, a secretary of a savings and loan association, and said: "Al, on the basis of what I know you believe, I'd like you to set aside a quarter of a million dollars exclusively for making home loans to Negroes."

After I pointed out to him that some of the Negro home buyers were among the best risks in the city, he agreed. When he used up the quarter million, he allocated more. As a result more savings and loan associations opened their doors to Negroes and helped them break out of their ghetto.

Though Negroes in our city are still circumscribed, and a lot of new physical and moral frontiers have yet to be pierced, we did help make a small start. In doing our duty as we saw it, we disturbed the status quo, and made some people uncomfortable. But isn't it true that as we move from the old to the new, there is bound to be some resistance? We cannot grow without a clash of opinion.

BUILDING AN IMAGE

Creating a business image is like composing a symphony or painting a picture. There has to be an over-all concept along with the supporting detail. If you permit your business to unravel aimlessly, it will sag and snag—its public image will be poor. However, if you have a design and support it with responsible specific action, the resulting favorable image can be of inestimable value.

One of our moves in attempting to build a good image was to adopt the slogan: "We are a dependable real estate institution." We then set out to earn our claim. To create an atmosphere of reliability we engaged an attorney who specialized in real estate law to close our deals. This put our buyers and sellers at ease as they watched him handle the many legal details with poise and professional skill. In choosing men to represent our firm, we looked for dependability rather than glibness—men who wore well rather than those with glamorous personalities.

We did several other things to construct a favorable image. For instance, we set aside several thousand dollars a year which we call "mad money." We use it at deal closings wherever we encounter situations in which the buyer or seller becomes so rigid in his demands that the only alternative left to close the gap between them is to use some of our "mad money." Those dollars built reservoirs of good will for us. Unfortunately, there are some hard-to-reason-with people who see only black and white, and when these become fired up with righteous indignation, they can wreck deals. Our "mad money" has not only prevented many of our deals from falling apart, but by minimizing friction, it has helped build our image as a firm easy to deal with.

One day a couple came to our office and asked for me. The woman was weeping, and the man's face was a frozen picture of hostility. They had given a $500 down payment on a property the day before to one of my salesmen, and now, after a sleepless night, had decided not to go through with the deal.

"What's troubling you?" I asked when they were seated in my office.

"We changed our minds about buying the house from you," the woman said in a weepy voice. "We'd like to have half of our $500 back. We can't afford to lose it all.

"Ma'am," I said, "you can have all of your $500 back." The woman's face lit up. She wiped away her tears and said, "Oh, thanks, mister." The husband walked over and pumped my hand in gratitude.

Before they left I said, "If you should find another home we have for sale that you like better, we would be glad to sell it to you." They nodded their heads as they walked out.

I called the salesman who handled the deal and told him to stay with them. Eventually, he not only sold them another home, but through their good will our firm was able to complete four other sales.

Such details build up an image. The good will created by tiny good deeds is of inestimable value. Not to grasp opportunities to invest in good deeds, however insignificant, is like an artist omitting necessary detail needed to give his picture the impact he desires.

The local newspaper can be your friend if you know how to make use of it, or it can be your foe, if you are careless in the way you treat people. Many real estate transactions throb with poignant human interest stories. If you sell a home that has been lived in by one of the famous pioneers of your city, it's news. People in your community want to know about it. And if you don't submit such facts to your local newspaper, you are depriving readers of interesting news and not taking advantage of an opportunity to enhance your business image.

We traded one of our client's homes six times over a period of ten years—more often than some people trade their cars. The *Milwaukee Journal* thought it was a pretty good story. Our home trading division received publicity which was far more valuable than blowing our own horn in one of our ads. A favorable news story is far more effective than any ad.

When one of our top salesmen sold thirteen homes in one month, our newspaper ran it as a real estate news item. It helped build a man's confidence, as well as the prestige of the firm he worked for. The advertising value of the story was worth thousands of dollars to us.

It is not often that a salesman can sell a million dollars worth of real estate in one year. When one of our men did it, we saw to it that the newspaper found out about it. His picture was in the paper along with a column-long article giving a profile of the salesman, and some of the human interest details involved in building this enviable sales record. Such a feature story paves the way for more deals for the salesman, and opens new doors to his employer.

An image doesn't happen—it's created. If you want an image of integrity you have to perform deeds of integrity, and communicate them creatively. If you want to be known as a dependable real estate institution, you cannot afford to let any opportunity slip past to demonstrate your dependability.

A newspaper can be your ally or your enemy. It is your ally as long as your dealings are above board and you can point to instance after instance to confirm it. If you become careless and allow misrepresentation to gain a foothold in your organization, the newspaper can be quick to pounce on you and hurt you. Its intention may not be to harm you deliberately, but often the reporting of a minor offense can be blown out of proportion into a damaging story. Your protection from such adverse publicity is to be constantly on guard against sloppy representation and having an unflagging interest in the meticulous handling of your clients' interests. You help build a good image by not making mistakes which create a bad one.

DIRECTING MEN

Skillfully blueprinting a salesman's time and channeling his efforts in the right direction are part of successful management. Good management is taking the time to plan the best course of action and inspire others to follow it.

A prospective salesman is always impressed when we point out to him that there are at least twenty ways in which we could involve him in selling real estate. Usually he is surprised that there are so many. He respects us because of our specialized knowledge. This makes him depend on us, and hence he is easier to manage.

I suppose it should not be surprising that few salesmen are aware of the many ways open to them to get into the real estate business. To match the salesman with the approach most suitable to develop his potentialities is an extremely important decision for management, and crucial for the salesman. Often it can mean the difference between failure, mediocrity, or leadership.

Singly or in combination, each of the following ways have been used by our salesmen to become successfully involved in the real estate business.

Every new salesman should make a list of friends, relatives and acquaintances of no fewer than three hundred names, the more the better, and announce through a personal letter that he is qualified to handle their real estate needs. Those who do not painstakingly compile this list and advertise their readiness to serve are passing up thousands of dollars in potential commissions. Few take advantage of this obvious and most effective first step to get launched into a real estate career.

It is safe to offer any pleasant, intelligent, dependable-looking salesman a draw of $4,000 a year against commissions, if he agrees to canvass house-to-house four hours a day for real estate listings. This is a sure-fire, result-getting method if a certain area of ten or twenty square blocks is staked out, and the salesman makes it his responsibility personally to meet and talk to every homeowner within the designated neighborhood. It is difficult work but the results are almost guaranteed.

The pleasant problem that arises out of this approach is that the salesman soon becomes so involved in listing, showing, and selling interviews, that he can't spare the four hours a day to continue the canvassing. Those who have robust health and like to meet new people are more likely to be successful in canvassing. The introvert, the dreamer and the person in delicate health is least likely to be a successful canvasser.

Every good-sized city prints a directory listing the names and telephone numbers of home owners. Some people with pleasant voices are more convincing on the telephone than in person. Over the years we have had several men who made $6,000 to $8,000 a year regularly from the leads they obtained by making twenty to thirty cold turkey phone calls daily. It is hard, tedious work, and only the hardy souls who can reconcile themselves to the tedium succeed.

Many owners of property bypass the broker and attempt to sell their real estate themselves. They either put out "For Sale By Owner" signs or advertise their homes in their local newspapers. Salesmen can make a good living by following up these leads and persuading the owners that selling real estate is highly specialized work, and that they could best protect their interests by listing their properties with a highly trained and reputable organization. Several men in our firm have consistently earned $10,000 to $12,000 a year by concentrating on this approach.

Unfortunately, a certain number of people lose their homes in foreclosure. Most cities or counties print this information in the vital statistics column. By viewing the property, talking to the mortgagee and the mortgagor, an alert salesman can "sniff" out enough good deals during the year to make profitable the time he spends following up these leads. This method appeals only to the patient pursuer of facts. He must be willing to spend countless hours with the principals, attorneys and government file clerks, patiently hoping that one out of ten or twenty foreclosures will have enough leeway left to enable him to make a profit between the total foreclosed indebtedness and what he eventually can get for the property.

Joining civic and service organizations may not be a direct way of becoming involved in selling real estate, but when combined with one or two other methods it can become an important adjunct. A real estate salesman must mingle with people. The more he can stretch himself among his acquaintances, the more calls and tips he'll get from them. The camaraderie that develops between members of clubs and organizations creates an atmosphere of trust and reliability—an asset that the alert salesman can convert into money in the bank.

The following aid to selling applies to those who are already successful but want to improve their sales volume. The salesman who takes the time to write a personal letter to each buyer and seller, thanking him for the privilege of serving him, and makes it his business to pay periodic visits to all those who bought properties from him, is making an investment in friendship that will build reservoirs of good will, and commissions for the future. Few salesmen do it in spite of its guaranteed effectiveness. It is a friendly way of building a clientele which will not deal with anyone but you.

Some men are better suited to deal with the classes and some are better fitted to deal with the masses. Some are at their best selling Cadillacs, others selling Fords. We have some salesmen who earn $10,000 to $15,000 a year selling low priced homes. They would be flops trying to sell luxury homes to executives. It is important for management to direct its men where they are likely to be most effective.

One day I interviewed a vacuum cleaner salesman who was interested in joining our firm. I explained the various ways in which he could become involved. Trading properties appealed to him the most. When I explained the principals of trading, I could see his eyes light up with understanding. He and I made the right choice, because by concentrating on trading homes, he earned $20,000 during his first year with our organization.

A salesman can make a good living if he is willing to invest dozens of hours cultivating the good will of twenty to thirty savings and loan secretaries, and become their trouble shooter in disposing of their foreclosed properties, or better still, in nipping foreclosure in the bud by solving through sales the problems of their heavily delinquent accounts.

Selling new homes requires specialized knowledge, and the salesman who learns the rudiments of construction and becomes proficient in comparative values can become an expert in selling new homes for builders. Several of our salesmen have made lucrative clients out of small builders who knew how to build but did not know how to sell. Large builders usually have their own sales organizations.

The residential building boom of the 1950's required the ingenuity of real estate salesmen to find the lots and acreage to feed the hungry builders. Several of our salesmen spent most of their time specializing in selling lots and raw land, and then persuading builders to list their new homes with our firm because we had the specialists who knew how to sell them. Special knowledge is required in this field, and the salesman who takes the time to learn it can often make more money than the mill run home salesman.

We have three men who apply themselves exclusively to selling investment property. To sell a multi-family apartment building, a shopping center, a factory or an office building requires specialized knowledge—a knowledge to intelligently compare real estate rates of return with the returns on other types of investments. A real estate investment specialist must be not only mathematically inclined and have the ability to handle executive caliber men, but also must have broad economic knowledge, especially as it relates to tax law and real estate depreciation. A salesman in this category should not consider himself successful unless he is able to sell between $500,000 to $1,000,000 of real estate a year.

A source of real estate commissions which will be on the increase in the future is selling foreclosed properties for the Federal Housing and Veterans Administrations. Hundreds of millions of dollars worth of homes have been and will be foreclosed by these government agencies, and the real estate salesmen who will take the time to learn the red-tape rules of these bureaucracies will be the ones to sell them. The real estate broker who does not avail himself of this huge reservoir of listings is letting commissionable opportunities slip through his fingers.

We have a salesman who has quietly gained the confidence of several dozen attorneys, and when any of them have to dispose of a property as a result of a divorce, a probate matter, or dividing an estate, he is called in to sell the real estate. Added to his other real estate involvements, the occasional bonanzas that come his way when his attorney friends call him often turn average years into highly successful ones.

Whenever we sell a home, we send a friendly card to the surrounding two or three square blocks of home owners calling attention to the fact that we have sold so-and-so's home at such-and-such address. We stress that we have several other prospects who would like to live in the same neighborhood. This is far more effective direct mail advertising than spraying a large area with general advertising. We channel the replies to our request for listings in a specific area to the salesman who sold the property in the area. Whenever possible, we have the salesman write and send out the cards to personalize the message.

Some men are more fatherly than others. They make good managers, often better managers than salesmen. Those who combine imagination, a flair for administration and the patience to listen and to solve salesmen's problems, are more valuable as managers than salesmen—to themselves and to their organization. We have been able to convert several undistinguished salesmen into top managers.

In addition to directing men in how they can involve themselves most successfully, we prepare a syllabus for each salesman suggesting how many cold turkey calls he should make daily, how many warm up calls, and how many property showings he should average a week.

It is management's responsibility to chart the way, and if it has that extra ingredient of being able to inspire, then, indeed, it is not only directing men, but building men.

6.

On Being Extraordinary—
Putting People Ahead of Profit

As I look back upon the opinions I have developed from my experiences in real estate, two stand out above all others. One is that *sincerity* is a far more effective selling tool than syllabuses and scientific selling kits. Arousing interest, creating desire, and closing sales techniques are less important than the dynamic force of sincerity.

The other is *originality*. They form a bold partnership. When linked together they melt the resistance that halts ordinary efforts. The combination transmutes humdrum activity into extraordinary endeavor.

I was fortunate to discover the dynamism of sincerity early in my real estate career. At the time of my graduation from the University of Wisconsin in 1933, I was an introvert dreamily hoping and planning to become a writer. For four years I was buffeted from failure to failure during the trying depression years. Because of the austere times, coupled with my inexperience as a writer, I was unable to find employment. In desperation I tried selling. I became a real estate salesman.

I was naïve, idealistic, impractical, and, to top it off, I had a poor sense of direction. Often when I called on a prospect to show him a property, I would get lost on the way, and when I admitted my inadequacy and asked for help, the prospect would willingly, almost with gusto, direct me to the home he wanted to see. This immediately developed a friendly relationship, and I caught the first glimpse of the power of raw sincerity as an aid to selling. I didn't offer excuses. I asked for help. It was putting sincerity to work.

In my naïve, impractical manner, I would point out home defects such as basement cracks, rusty gutters or a roof that needed repairs. I noticed that when I was completely honest about the minuses, the prospects would listen attentively when I called attention to an unusually bright dining room, a spacious living room or modern kitchen cabinets. When I told my buyers I could arrange financing on homes so that the monthly payments—interest, principal and taxes—would not be more than rent for the same type of accommodation, I could see in their eyes that they believed me. When I said that if they didn't like the properties I showed them I would make it my business to find exactly what they wanted, I discovered that they did not go to look elsewhere, but waited for me to make good my promise. When I responded to this loyalty with all the sincerity I could muster, I began making sales in spite of my inexperience. I soon realized that I was not so naïve and impractical as I had supposed. I had stumbled on a selling secret which gave me a power to persuade.

Sincerity not linked to action is just wasted energy. Sincerity untested in the heat of living ends up in soft naïveté. Sincerity coupled with originality and bold action can change an ordinary real estate man into an extraordinary one.

It's so tempting and comfortable to be an ordinary real estate man. Shortcuts and little expediencies often bring quick commissions. These quick successes are imperceptibly consolidated into a "profits first and people second" point of view, and the practitioners of such a "success at any cost" policy wind up leading empty and ordinary lives, though to the public they may appear dazzlingly successful. Spiritual dry rot starts in the person who decides to fool the public at the expense of his conscience.

How an ordinary salesman can become extraordinary

How can an ordinary real estate salesman become extraordinary? By convincing himself that he can make as great a contribution to society through his work as does the physician, minister, or lawyer.

A real estate man deals in the largest and most important single item of a family budget. By selling a home to a family which meets its needs, in a location it will be happy in, and on terms it can afford, a salesman can add to a family's health and peace of mind as much as any other individual. Conversely, the salesman who is more interested in his commission than in the people he deals with can create havoc in a family that is high-pressured into the wrong house, located in an incompatible neighborhood, or burdened with terms which create financial hardship.

A real estate salesman who sincerely regards his work with the reverence of a minister approaching his responsibilities to his parishioners is no longer an ordinary real estate man; he is an extraordinary man.

A real estate salesman sincerely meeting the basic needs of society can put his head on his pillow at night with more satisfaction than a bubble gum manufacturer, a whisky distributor, or a cigarette salesman. It is far more rewarding to sell to people what they need than to make money catering to their weaknesses.

It is not easy to put people ahead of profit. It requires courage and wisdom—the courage to let go of the little successes that come from putting profit ahead of people, and the wisdom to realize that the favor we get by bribing someone with a bottle of whisky erodes character. Expediencies accumulate and harden into a standardless point of view if we don't apply courage and wisdom. Without realizing it, our expediencies become normal and involuntary. We become "bad guys" without knowing it.

People admire knowledge but it pales in comparison to the hunger for trust. Most would rather deal with a sincere amateur they can trust than with a glib "smoothie" who knows all the answers. When a salesman makes a decision to be completely honest he not only arms himself with a powerful selling secret, but more important, he sets the stage for dedicated and purposeful living. Those who blind themselves with expediency can't see it. They are motivated only by short term results. The courageous and wise who stick to honest sincerity in spite of temporary failures eventually realize its long-term benefits.

Poetry sells a dream cottage

I was showing a cottage to an engaged couple late one afternoon. It was easy to see they were very much in love. After I had showed them the interior of the home, the three of us walked out to the rear yard. It was mid-June. The close cropped grass was freshly cut, and the borders of the rear lot were banked with a profusion of colorful flowers. There was a twilight hush in the air, that tip-toe time between the end of the day and the beginning of evening.

I was so enchanted by the exchange of the couple's amorous glances that I failed to notice whether they were being impressed by what I was showing them. I was so wrapped up in the mood they created that I neglected to do any selling. Suddenly I was struck by an impulse. It was to recite a stanza of poetry which I thought described the idyllic scene. I asked their permission. They smiled approvingly. I don't recall the words, but I do remember that when I finished, it didn't seem awkward or corny. The purity of their emotions and my sincerity seemed to merge into a genuine rapport. As we were walking back to our cars the young man said, "We like it. We want to buy it."

It was that simple.

A sincere health suggestion leads to a half million dollar trade

Sincerity and originality are an effective combination. Early in my real estate selling career I encountered a testy gentleman who owned thirty old cottages, duplexes and rooming houses which he had acquired through foreclosure on his mortgages. He was an arch conservative who cursed President Franklin Roosevelt without realizing that his liberal president was putting into effect economic policies which soon would double his real estate holdings.

Being high strung and nervous, he took a terrible mental beating every time he attempted to negotiate a sale on one of his properties. His plan was to sell his foreclosed residential real estate, re-invest the proceeds in a multifamily apartment building, and retire on its income. When he told me about it, I said to him:

"Mr. Johnson, would you be willing to take some sincere advice from a man a lot younger than you? You're one of those full-of-fight men who'd lose years of good health if you tried to sell each of your real estate parcels separately.

"I've got an idea that could help us both. I'll buy the 40 family apartment building that I know you have your eye on, and trade it with you for the 30 pieces of property you own. My organization will then take over the sale of your various properties, and hope to make five per cent or so above the purchase price.

"I know your first reaction will be: 'Why should I let him make the profit,' but what I can save you in health and bother would be worth it. And, by the way, we'd be legitimately earning our profit."

As I look back, it took a lot of originality, or perhaps a better word would be nerve, for a youngster like me to advise an opinionated oldster like Mr. Johnson. But I struck a responsive chord.

Several days later he came to my office and said, "George, I've thought it over. I'll take your advice."

For a week we locked horns over terms, and when the dickering was resolved we both sighed with relief. The trade deal would never have been made had he not had complete trust in me. My sincerity overcame his mountainous resistance. It gave me the help to deal with a difficult man.

Mr. Johnson is in his early eighties now, and spends his winters in Florida retired on the income from the forty-family apartment building I sold him. It was my first bold move in real estate. It worked out well for him, and for me.

Success—difficult to handle

We live in a time when too many halos are put on success and not enough on the means by which it is attained. Those who are success-motivated have greater difficulty taming their wills than those who use success as a means to lead more purposeful lives. Success without finding something bigger to live for confounds, compromises, and confuses its victims. No wonder there are so many "successful" failures.

I know many men in the real estate business who are being torn apart by success. They are financially fat on the outside and starving from lack of purpose on the inside.

I also know men who never attained financial success but are living successful lives. Because they found something big to live for they were able to turn ordinary circumstances into extraordinary opportunities.

Here are several thumbnail profiles of men who put profit ahead of people, and of some who put people ahead of profit.

WILLOUGHBY—A SUCCESSFUL FAILURE

Willoughby's insatiable desire to get the best of a deal brought him success and hostility. He connived and manipulated to get 103 per cent out of every deal, and salved his conscience by calling it efficiency, instead of graciously taking 97 per cent, and building goodwill. He made millions.

His incisive mind was able to cut to the heart of a deal in a few minutes, and he was as swift to carve out the best part of it for himself. He always wanted an edge, and he usually got it. The irony of it is that it would have cost him little, compared to what he was worth, to have been gracious instead of hard. To give an edge rather than take one doesn't cost much.

Willoughby paid the price for pushing for ends without caring for means. People feared and disliked him. Dislike is always a companion of fear.

His image in his community kept plummeting as fast as his financial success was rising. He was smart enough to stay within the law but not wise enough to avoid becoming a first rate scoundrel.

Willoughby was poised, confident and cocky on the outside, and purposeless on the inside. He had nothing to give to his fellow man. How could he give when he tried to wring the best for himself out of every situation?

When one's attitude is bent on taking, it makes him unfit to give, even to his family. Willoughby gave his wife and children a palatial home, food fit for royalty, and money to satisfy their every whim, but he starved them for what money couldn't buy—sincerity and love. He had none to give.

In real life it is not easy to play Dr. Jekyll and Mr. Hyde roles. If one is generous all day in business, it's second nature for him to be generous at home. If he's tight-fisted during the day it's difficult to open his hands in a giving gesture at night. Willoughby couldn't do it, nor can anyone else.

OLIVER—HE GAVE TO GET A DOUBLE DIVIDEND

Oliver was head of a bank's trust department in charge of real estate investments. His job was to advise clients when to sell their real estate, when and what to buy, and to so manage their property as to get the highest rate of return.

Having dealt with hard hitting entrepreneurs who too often eager-beavered their way into personal fortunes based on what the traffic will bear, it was refreshing to watch Oliver work enthusiastically for the welfare of others. I dealt with him often. He was far more informed than many of the enterprisers he dealt with, yet he was content to use his talents for others rather than accumulate wealth for himself.

"You know five times as much as some of those who are in business for themselves," I told him one day as we philosophized between deals. "How come you never went into the real estate business for yourself?"

"There's more *giving* in my work," he replied. "There's too much *getting* when one's in business for himself. I don't want to condemn entrepreneurs, but for me, I know I can derive more satisfaction in advising others on how to make money, than getting involved in the storms of trying to make it for myself."

Oliver regarded his work with reverence. I felt more secure in Oliver's promise than in a signed contract with some of the entrepreneurs I dealt with. Oliver's basic attitude was to be uncompromisingly fair. He ran his life on the basis of absolute moral standards, not often used by men who are guided primarily by success.

Oliver was a keen real estate analyst as well as a practical theologian. He enjoyed drawing parallels between his work and the way he wanted to live. In one of our discussions he made an observation which was one of the most cogent I had ever heard. He said:

"I believe that living a moral life is the most practical approach to living. By doing good one clips coupons while on earth, but equally and perhaps more important, he has a better chance of clipping coupons on the next level of consciousness as well. Why should one be so foolish as to risk closing his mind to life after death when he has no way of proving it? Why should one cynically ask for proof of life after death, rather than joyously believe in it, until it is definitely disproved? It makes more sense to be optimistic than pessimistic."

Out of Oliver's spiritual commitment evolved a practical and extraordinary real estate man.

WILEY—HE SETTLED FOR PEANUTS

When Wiley was clerking in a department store he had to be content with make believe about what he would do when he became wealthy. After a series of changes in which he left his job, gambled his savings successfully in real estate, and pyramided his earnings as prosperous times carried him aloft, his dreams became realities.

For some, wealth leads to maturity and responsibility. In Wiley's case it led to whisky and women. His flaunted immorality was a disgrace to his family and community. But because of his money power he neutralized both, so that he was neither rejected nor accepted. His generous charitable contributions enabled him to obtain lukewarm acceptability, and by showering his family with all they wanted, he managed to blunt their rejection. His wife and children did not love him, they endured him.

Wiley's desires swelled with his wealth. Desires undisciplined by something big to live for can twist a man into unnatural living. Wiley's direct goals were to make profitable real estate deals, and with their earnings to feed his insatiable desires for lewd and conspicuous indulgence. His real estate activities created jobs, but he did not build men. He helped tear them down. As he moved from one deal to another he stepped on the less competent and adroitly sidestepped those who were more knowledgeable and ruthless than he. By studiously and shrewdly staying within the law he was a greater menace to his community than the less calculating ones who break the law and get caught.

Though Wiley's exterior had a thin veneer of respectability, he was full of dry rot inside. He didn't reach for experiences that satisfied the heart. He settled for those that satisfied the senses. His wealth gave him an opportunity to transcend himself. Instead he descended into depravity.

Measured by standards more meaningful than Wiley set for himself, the rewards of his success turned into ashes. The power of money not only eroded his moral standards, but contorted his face into a lewd expression of stealthy consumption.

What happened to Wiley can happen to unwary real estate entrepreneurs who are catapulted into success. Though they become experts in making money they become foolish in the use of it. Instead of reaching for pearls, they settle for peanuts.

ORVILLE—HIS CLIENTS ARE HIS PATIENTS

Orville is unheralded and unseen. He's not the glittering kind. No one raves about the cement in a beautiful building, but without its binding power the building would crumble. Orville was the cement, the binding energy in his community.

Orville sells about fifty homes a year without the aid of salesmen. He serves his clients with the same concern with which a good family doctor dotes on his patients. Orville makes every real estate sale a personalized, caring experience. His clients become his friends. The commercial aspect of the relationship is subordinated as he counsels, advises and arranges the housing needs of the people he deals with.

Orville is not a leader. He is a worker. He is not in the limelight in his local Real Estate Board, nor is he influential at the real estate conventions he attends. But without his unselfish and quiet devotion to work, his Real Estate Board would not function as well, nor would the conventions he attends go off on schedule.

Orville gives hundreds of hours during the year to make his local Real Estate Board an effective force for good in his profession, and hundreds of hours at conventions outside his city, to help men share their knowledge, to serve better, and earn more. Orville doesn't grace the head tables, nor does he seek attention to become better known. He is most content when he can work quietly without applause or commendation.

Orville does not have the eager beaver look. He makes no effort to elbow himself into recognition. He is naturally friendly, and those who take the time to look at him more closely, as I did, find serenity in depth. This is understandable because, instead of straining at the leash to get, Orville has decided that the natural way to live is to give.

Orville's mind does not yearn for the rarefied financial heights where the real estate tycoons climb and stumble. But what Orville stakes out for himself, he not only does well, but healingly touches the lives of those he deals with.

Would Orville still be the joy of his clients if he climbed the soaring heights of real estate success? It is difficult to tell. The temptations that success brings in its wake could corrupt fine men like Orville. I have seen it happen. That's why it's important to discipline our increasing freedoms. Increasing freedom, unwisely used, can become a curse instead of a blessing.

The Orvilles ennoble the real estate profession. They find the secret of natural commitment to good, and in the process of quietly putting it to work serving their fellow men, they become extraordinary.

WEBSTER—A LITTLE ROBBER BARON

Webster was a minor league robber baron who schemed and elbowed his way to success. He climbed beyond his business ability and capacity to handle success, and his face showed it. His shifty eyes and furtive glances became involuntary. He could no longer control them. They were the result of years of wheeling and dealing in which he allowed hard bargaining, corner cutting, and ruthlessness to dominate him.

He didn't deal in millions or in hundreds of thousands. His deals were small. He dealt with the less sophisticated. He dealt harshly. He always seemed to be out of breath when he talked, gulping down air between phrases, and pushing his points of view with his hands and face.

I bought a property from Webster years ago when we were both getting started. He let me see a signed contract showing that he had paid $15,000 for a rooming house. All he wanted, he said, was $1,000 profit. I agreed to pay $16,000. Several months later I had an occasion to meet the man who sold Webster the rooming house. In the course of our conversation I learned that Webster bought the property for $13,000 instead of $15,000. When I confronted Webster with the lie and said, "Web, that was a fake contract you showed when you sold me the rooming house," he replied evasively, "I bet you'll still make a profit on it."

"But you're smart enough to make money the right way. Why do you have to stoop to faking contracts?"

"It convinced you, didn't it?"

"But I won't believe you the next time," I said.

"We'll worry about next time when it happens."

Webster was shrewd enough not to get outside the law, but he often skirted close to its borders. He kicked up a lot of dust. And it got in the eyes of the people he dealt with. His driving ambition and hard work brought him success but at the double price of stirring up a tornado inside him and the backlash effect on others.

Webster was an example of how human nature can take a turn and go on a rampage, interfering in the affairs of others. Braving the danger of moralizing, I suggested to him one day that if he disciplined his energy by making it honest he could make a contribution to his community, instead of irritating it with his grasping methods. His reply was astonishingly honest and blunt.

"I'm honest 80 per cent of the time. For instance, I'm honest with you when I admit this. Some lie more than I, and never admit it. I don't have wings sprouting out of my shoulders, but when a guy can be 80 per cent honest, it's not so bad."

"But as long as you're willing to be 80 per cent honest, would it cost you so much to go all the way?"

"Yes, I'd lose too many deals. Perhaps when I become wealthy and have complete security, I'll give myself the luxury of going honest all the way. Until then, better keep your hand in your pocket, at least 20 per cent of the time."

It was difficult to get angry with a man like that. He was a puzzling menace. He was bent into dishonesty out of twisted motives—to grasp what he could get away with. He gave the principle of private enterprise a black eye. He made Karl Marx look good. Private enterprisers like Webster, who damn socialism, don't realize they help bring it on by the way they live and do business.

ALBERT—A PRINCE OF PRIVATE ENTERPRISE

Albert made success look easy. He had none of the strain that comes from climbing to the top. He reached dizzying heights of real estate dealing, yet remained clear-headed and sure-footed. Success and money didn't corrupt his character. They enhanced it. What was his secret?

Before revealing it, let me sketch a few more lines. He is neither soft nor firm within his one hundred men real estate organization. He emphasizes wisdom rather than authority. He not only tells those who work for him how to do their work, but why they should do it well. It was in explaining the whys that he became inspirational and converted ordinary into extraordinary men.

Albert builds, manages, sells and buys real estate in cities across the length and breadth of America. He is both dreamer and doer. He nourishes others with imaginative plans, and has converted several of his own ideas into concrete realities. Wherever he creates work he builds goodwill.

In spite of his business activities, speaking engagements and devotion to civic and charitable organizations, he is a relaxed father and husband. This is a feat more difficult than becoming a tycoon. He doesn't bring the rush of business to his family because there is no rush in his makeup. He is a conduit through which work flows at an even pace.

His wealth is in the millions. But his success was not in accumulating it, but having the wisdom to put it to its highest and best use. Albert used his wealth to fill men's hands with work, and he did it in such a manner that it also satisfied their hearts. He accomplished the latter by adding the inspirational factor *why* to the technical *how*.

What is Albert's secret which did not allow his wealth to

debilitate his character? I have talked to him, and I am convinced that it is because he takes direction for his life from a well reasoned Christian base. His humility and sincerity stem from a God-guided man. He doesn't talk about it, he lives it. He was meek, but when someone mistook it for softness and tried to take advantage of him, they felt his steel. When I questioned him about modern theological ideas he quickly told me he didn't fool with any form of humanism, ethical culture, or existentialism. He said:

"My consciousness is rooted in an intelligence far transcending my own. I call it God. And just as a drop of water is one with the ocean so am I one with Him. My job is to translate this relationship into practical living."

Albert has done it. His passion for Christianity is greater than his desire to indulge in his wealth. His greater passion blocked out the lesser one. Only an ultimate passion can quiet a lesser passion.

Men of Albert's stature build men. They do not exploit. They are the men of tomorrow who can effectively give the lie to Karl Marx's contention that private enterprise must die because it breeds selfishness in men who corrupt themselves in the use of their power. Men like Albert are more revolutionary than the Communists. They start a revolution for good in their own hearts, instead of imposing it forcefully on others.

Private enterprise not only can win against Communism, but change it, with men like Albert, Orville and Oliver. We can lose to Communism when a vacuum is created by a general retreat of character led by men like Willoughby, Wiley and Webster.

Private enterprise is like nuclear power

Private enterprise brings out the best in men, ideas, and products. Competition develops excellence. A real estate project under private enterprise must make economic sense and satisfy people or it cannot succeed. In a collective socialistic society, projects do not have to meet these tests. That's why socialism imposes unimaginative drabness on its people. Its products are second rate. Its ideas are stilted. The wall dividing East and West Berlin dramatizes the contrast between the anemic efforts of an incentive-sterilized society, and the virility where excellence and imagination are encouraged to flourish.

But we cannot smugly rest on the laurels of this comparison. Private enterprise, used unselfishly, can lead to glorious heights of self-expression; if used selfishly, it can destroy us.

Private enterprise is like nuclear power. It can be used for good to give men the comforts of a highly evolved civilization, or it can be exploited to tear the free world apart.

Wherever economic selfishness and political dishonesty are allowed to run rampant, collectivism of the left or fascism of the right takes over. Responsible men of America, England, France, Italy and the Scandinavian countries have staved off monolithic takeover by creatively finding peaceful means with which to distribute the wealth within their countries, and giving more freedom to their people. As long as enlightened leaders through enlightened legislation sincerely work toward minimizing exploitation and maximizing economic and political freedom, Communism will not only be held at bay, it can be rolled back in the countries that have it. If we condemn ourselves to live selfishly, we will not only have collectivism, but we will deserve it.

When building character becomes the goal of the many and practicing corruption that of an aberrant few, then people create the climate for victorious living under private enterprise, and the people of Communist countries will want it too. It's the only way we can change them—not by force, which they know how to use more ruthlessly than we.

It is pointless for conservatives to beat their breasts for freedom, and then try to hide behind the Constitution to deprive some people of its blessings. And it is pointless for liberals to recite idealistic slogans if their central motive in promoting a welfare state is to get more collectivized power, and not because helping people is the Christian thing to do.

The aim of conservatives and liberals alike must be to find a purpose in life big enough to transcend secondary political and economic motives. When that happens all else falls properly in place.

Men in real estate are engaged in important work. It is the biggest industry in America. How we conduct ourselves will determine what happens to us, to our community, to our nation, and to the world. We can put ourselves to our highest and best use, or become like the "white elephant" properties that some of us get stuck with—obsolete and of no use.

7.

Real Estate of Tomorrow

Real estate concerns our basic needs. It shapes our most elemental habits. What and how we build molds our physical environment.

Man's need for shelter has been functionalized by caves and romanticized by cathedrals. Out of advanced technology we created new real estate forms to meet our increasingly complex needs. Can we peer into the future and see the outlines of things to come—the real estate of the future?

Responsible real estate men of tomorrow will have to create shelter which will satisfy people instead of merely producing high rates of return. Imagine what would happen to medical research if medical science were interested only in commercializing its knowledge! Is it asking for the moon to expect real estate men to dedicate themselves to their profession with the same devotion that men of medicine do?

Planning based on putting profits ahead of people leads to quick obsolescence and slum formation. Irresponsible real estate men thus contribute to human misery. By parasitically preying on their communities to see how much they can suck out of them, real estate men create inferior shelter which can sadden and saddle their children and grandchildren for several decades.

To meet the needs of a complex society, private and public enterprise must form a harmonious partnership. Private enterprise with its flair for freedom will have to play its role imaginatively against a backdrop of public planning. Too much planning without the spark of private enterprise will only get us the unimaginative drabness of a collective society. Too much private enterprise without regard to public welfare brings about the criticism and public interference that private enterprise wishes to avoid.

Real estate of tomorrow must meet the test of economic feasibility, as well as giving satisfaction to people. Here are some new real estate forms which meet the tests of both.

Wildwood Village

Only the most hardened urbanites do not reminisce wistfully about roaming the country fields, walking through shady lanes, or climbing flower covered hills. There is a way to turn these memories into realities.

A broker friend of mine, with whom I often philosophized, and who knew my thoughts on combining the practical with the idealistic, came to my office one day, his face alive with excitement.

"George," he said, "I found a thirty acre tract that's a dream. It's so heavily wooded that when you're deep in trees you'd think you're in the wilds of Canada. Its rolling hills are like those of Virginia. And what makes it so ideal, it's only twenty minutes from the center of downtown. You've asked me to be on the lookout for something like this. Well, I've found it."

I drove out to see it that same afternoon. I was enchanted. The owner had kept it as a natural preserve. He had built several rustic bridges connecting the gently rolling hills, and in addition to a stream that coursed through his land, he created an artificial lake. As I trampled over the crackling twigs underneath the huge old trees, I was reminded of scenes in the movie "Brigadoon" set in Scotland's thickly wooded heather country.

As I was driving back to my office a plan was forming in my mind. I was unable to do my administrative work that afternoon. While the excitement of the wooded scene still occupied my thoughts, I began to put down on paper the feasibility of building a village near a metropolitan city.

Within several days I had in mind the general outline of my plan. I would build 300 apartments on the thirty acres—four buildings with 75 apartments in each. The woods would be left intact, except for an area to be carved out for the structures and parking. One building would cater to senior citizens who could afford eighty dollars a month rent for a 550 square foot, one-bedroom unit. A short distance away I planned another 75 apartments containing two-bedroom units catering to another group of elderly couples who could afford to pay one hundred and five dollars a month. Several blocks away, connected by scenic wooded lanes, would be the two other buildings. They were to be built on the opposite shores of the small lake, and were to consist of two- and three-bedroom apartments intended for younger couples with families who could afford from $110 to $125 a month rent.

My plan called for Swiss chalet motif architecture, generous use of fieldstone and red cedar on the exteriors, and simple, austere lines for the interiors. The central theme of the design was to blend the buildings into the forested environment.

It would be called Wildwood Village.

The special amenities for the senior citizens would be: a library, card room, snack bar, commissary, prayer room, crafts area and a large recreation hall. For outdoor activities I planned a shuffleboard court, a horseshoe pitching area, and a putting green. Management was to provide nightly activities in the public areas for those who wanted to participate. These would consist of lectures, dances, movies, card playing, and free coffee and cookies several times a week. My plan called for management to seek out the lonely couples and tactfully attempt to draw them into the village social center.

The special amenities for the two 75-apartment buildings catering to the interests of the younger families would be tennis courts, a baseball diamond and an equipped playground for small tots. A party room large enough to seat all the tenants in the two buildings was to be provided, and so designed that it could be divided by a movable partition into two areas, one for adults and the other for their children.

I planned to make the lake located in the center of the woods the centerpiece of the village. By stocking it with fish I would make it a haven for the fishing enthusiasts. On its shores I planned a free-standing building to contain a snack bar, a hot room, a steam room, and a men's conversation room with a pot bellied stove in the center of it to simulate the "good old days" when men relaxed and chewed the fat. And for the women, I planned a large bright room where they could knit, sew and kaffeeklatsch.

The central theme of Wildwood Village would be to bring back the atmosphere and leisure of bygone days. Parents could send their children to spend the night on a hill in a tent several blocks away, yet be within the thirty-acre village. Neighbors could visit each other walking along forest trails, and the more hearty ones could short cut through the underbrush. The factory or office workers coming home in the late afternoon could relax on the lake shore in the sun during the summer, or—if they dared—roll in the snow in the winter after a steam bath in the 180° Finnish sauna room. It would be bringing a bit of old leisurely Europe to Wildwood Village.

This type of residential planning is far superior to building row upon row of four- or eight-family buildings with their barracklike look and their lack of the special and social amenities that can add so much interest to apartment living. To offer shelter alone today is not enough. It becomes obsolete the day it is built.

Can Wildwood Village, with all its countrylike appeal and amenities, be made economically feasible? Yes. I estimated the cost of the three hundred apartments, including all the public areas, and allowing $100,000 for the thirty acres, to be $3,000,-000. Before I turned this project over to an architect, I had a $3,000,000 tentative conventional loan commitment, as well as FHA interest in the same amount if I wanted to grapple with its red tape.

My estimated income from the 300 apartments was $425,000 a year. Interest and principal amortization on $3,000,000 at the rate of 6 per cent for 25 years was about $230,000 a year. I estimated taxes and other fixed expenses to be about $150,000 a year. This left a cushion of about $45,000 a year of cash overage—not bad for practically no investment except eighteen months of planned excitement and hard work.

By the time I had assembled this housing idea in all its countrylike detail, I was too occupied with other ventures to go ahead with it. However, because Wildwood Village was so well packaged, I had no problem in selling the idea and the land to an entrepreneur, and with a few improvisations he built the project as I had envisioned it.

Wildwood Village was conceived in a conversation with a broker about the problem of combining idealism and practical business principles. It led to the broker's showing me the ideal site. The fact that it was built by another doesn't matter. What matters is that it was built—that good ideas have legs, that they travel, and are materialized.

At the edge of every city are wooded areas which, if imaginatively developed, could offer a joyous way of life to thousands. If half a dozen Wildwood Villages were built in this country as a result of what I have described here, I would feel rewarded. What's more important, thousands of families would be grateful.

Back to the small town

The physical environment in which people live and work is molded more by real estate men than any other group. We are responsible for the quaint towns and well ordered cities, as well as the megalopolises which are dehumanizing us with their ant hill societies.

Is there an irreversible trend toward huge concentrations of people? Are the economic advantages of crowding people together going to dictate how man lives, even despite his wishes?

The revolution against megalopolis has already begun. The evidence is in the exodus of millions to the suburbs. But suburban living is only a partial answer. In fact, it has created new problems, including that bugaboo of commuting.

Let me dramatize it. I met with several officials of the Chicago and Northwestern Railroad in Chicago one day to discuss the possibility of leasing air rights over their railroad tracks in downtown Milwaukee. It was 4:30 P.M. when I left their office. As I stepped out on the street, thousands of white collar workers spilled out of the cavernous office buildings near by. Men and women made a beeline for the waiting commuter trains. It was not a time for leisurely walking, but I stopped for a moment and watched. I looked into the eyes of the people as they rushed past me. They were frighteningly impersonal. Each person maneuvered to get past the others, the men in their loping strides, the women with their quick staccato steps. The immediate goal of each was a seat on the train.

I joined the throng because I, too, wanted to get a seat for my ride back to Milwaukee. There was no gallantry on the train. Men vied with women for a place to sit. Within seconds after the train's starting lurch, most of the passengers had their noses buried in their newspapers.

The experience shook me. I began to wonder how many men and women caught in this daily rat race would be willing to forego the high pressures of megalopolis living for the more leisurely pace of a small town. Was there something that I, as a real estate man, could do?

I started a Back-To-The-Small-Town Division in my real estate firm to see what I could do in reversing the explosion toward huge population concentrations. I have not started a prairie fire in my state of Wisconsin, but I have done a few things which, if others would do likewise, could halt, and perhaps reverse, the trend toward ant hill living.

A man from a large city came to my office one day and told me that his doctor had recommended that he sell his restaurant and supermarket, and settle in a small town. The man was on the verge of a nervous and physical breakdown. His real estate and chattel mortgages totaled $80,000. He was delinquent in all accounts. I informed him he had about $10,000 equity in his holdings. I bought his restaurant and supermarket from him for $90,000, and had him invest his $10,000 in a small town lake resort in northern Wisconsin, subject to a $35,000 mortgage with low monthly payments. I later re-sold his properties to other operators for $100,000.

The fresh northern air perked up the new resort owner as water perks up a wilted flower. Within a year, with his big city know-how, he not only made a success of his resort, but became a big man in local politics. He came to visit me one day and pumped my hand with such enthusiasm and gratitude that I hardly recognized him. He was a new man. He vibrated with new-found health.

"George," he said, "no job where I could make ten times

what I'm making could ever get me back to a large city. You've made me the happiest guy in the world. You're my friend for life."

I cannot heal the way a doctor can, but neither can a doctor heal the way I did. Healing takes many forms and can be applied in many ways by many kinds of people.

I didn't stop with an occasional sale. I called a conference of military personnel, large city industrialists, and several executives who had moved their businesses from large cities to small towns. The central theme of my remarks to the group was to induce the industrialists to decentralize some of their large city operations to the small towns of Wisconsin. The military representatives spoke favorably for the dispersal of industry. The small town business executives sang the praises of small town living.

The industrialists, however, listened and said nothing. They were concerned with economic laws, not with what would be good for the people in small towns. When the conference opened, my spirits soared. When it closed, they sank.

Undismayed, I spent a year gathering informative profiles on about thirty small towns of our state. I was invited to speak in several of them. The people were so warm to my ideas of bringing vital men and industry to their towns that they inspired me to hold on to my idea even though I was making little progress. As a result of my interest in small towns I partnered with another broker and built an 18-family apartment building in each of the following Wisconsin towns: Neenah, Appleton, Fond du Lac, Sheboygan, Oshkosh and Manitowoc. They were semiluxury, one-bedroom and efficiency units a block or two off the downtown area. They must have filled a need because they were rented as soon as we completed them.

I have placed some twenty small town businesses into stronger city hands. I know how eager the small towns are for commercial and industrial enterprises. If the industrialists can figure out a way to take their eyes off efficiency and economic laws, and put them on revitalizing democracy through decentralization, they would be making a tremendously patriotic contribution to their country.

Cities of the future

If we had a choice of distributing our 200,000,000 people in cities from 50,000 to 500,000, or concentrating them in huge megalopolises like Los Angeles, New York and Chicago, which ought we to choose? Grass root government may not be efficient in a small town, but neither does it have the built-in opportunities for corruption of the huge city. And it seems to me less corruption is more desirable than more efficiency.

Democracy has a better chance to flourish in towns and small cities of 50,000 to 500,000 than in megalopolises of five to ten million. We can slow down the senseless, feverish pace of big cities by encouraging an exodus to the small towns where the physical environment is more conducive to slower paced living.

We must be wise enough to put first things first. We don't have to let economic laws push us around. Doesn't it make sense to put the welfare of people first and economic laws second? Do we want people to live in a Los Angeles environment of city sprawl, and drive on its frightening freeways through a brown pall of smog, because economic laws work best in such an asphalt jungle atmosphere? Perhaps it makes economic sense, but it certainly doesn't make common sense. Does it make sense to concentrate 250,000 people in three and a half square miles of Harlem and dehumanize them in compressed squalor, while we still have hundreds of thousands of miles of wide open spaces? Something can be done if industrialists, businessmen and real estate men begin putting the interests of people first and economic laws second. Isn't it natural to want to spend our lives in a physical environment which enhances human dignity instead of debasing it?

Decades ago, men left the towns to make their mark in large cities. The towns in those days had no vitality or culture. People with ability left them to pour their talents into building the big cities. But now, many of them are trapped in a big city environment more debasing than the cultureless villages they left behind.

We need a master national plan to stop disgraceful urban sprawl and to revitalize the small towns. When we build new communities we ought to take a cue from the English and space green belts between them. We can afford them. They make sense. We have the land for this natural luxury.

As we connect the old and new cities along our superhighways, we ought to reserve several hundred yards on both sides of them for horseback riding, hiking, bicycling, and horse and buggy driving. We should have overnight hostels along these open dirt roads for those who want to make travel itself an enjoyment rather than concentrate on speed to get somewhere.

We must get a new concept of time. What's the point of becoming so efficient that we can build a skyscraper, let's say, in six months, or have an IBM computer send out a million bills in one hour, if in the speed we lose something more precious than we gain by beating time?

I remember an incident in Hawaii when a vacationing Los Angeles builder said to one local real estate man, as he looked up the slope of a mountain near Diamond Head: "If I were building here, I could subdivide that mountain, and sell all the homes in one year."

The Hawaiian looked at the fast talking mainlander and said with feeling: "I'm glad we don't have fellows like you here. You see, we want to enjoy our slower pace. What's wrong with taking five or ten years to build up the mountain?"

If industry decides to decentralize to make democracy work better, and disperses its vital people to the villages and small cities of America, the smaller and more orderly concentrations of people can make their communities interesting without the ant hill sordidness of the huge cities. Selective television programs, the ease with which one city's culture can be brought to another, and the ease with which people can travel from one place to another promote cultural leveling. Towns can have the intellectual ferment of the large city without its depersonalizing effects.

One of the most precious goals of man is to develop individuality. It is the central theme of our Constitution. It is the main reason we are against Communism. Yet we are in greater danger of losing our individuality to the huge cities than to Communism. Physical environment influences thinking. Real estate men and industrialists can shape our environment for good or evil. It depends on what they put first—people or profit.

Villages in the sky

City apartment living can be made more pleasant than it is today. Unfortunately, most apartment buildings are built with the motive of providing shelter at the highest rate of return to the investor. Cliff dwellers socialized more than the apartment dwellers do today, because they used the open spaces for public areas before they retired to their caves. Few of our apartment buildings have ample public areas for tenant socializing. Far too many of our structures are nondescript, imageless and characterless. And it is not surprising, because the main reason behind the construction of these buildings is not to offer a way of life, but to get the highest return on investment capital.

Why can't the apartments of the future be happy villages in the sky? They can be if the entrepreneur gives priority to the needs of people, or at least puts them on a par with the rate of return. In the long run, caring for tenants brings the highest rate of return in money, as well as the highest rate of return in the satisfaction of the heart. Free enterprise can be practical as well as idealistic if apartment planners keep their eyes on the most important ingredient—people. Too many of us think it is money!

If high rise apartments are to be happy villages in the sky, the grounds below must be beautiful and spacious. Allow each tenant the equivalent of a small back yard so that in a 100-family apartment building they will have a good-sized private park of their own. This type of zoning would decongest and beautify at the same time. Apartment owners should take as much pride in their parks as the English do in their gardens. Then the skyscrapers will make sense. They will have breathing space above and below. Skyscraper apartment buildings constructed on slivers of land in our large cities may make economic sense, but that's all. They don't make good living sense.

The apartments of the future should have breathing space not only externally but internally as well. Why can't they have public recreation areas where tenants can gather in the evening, snack bars, card rooms, libraries, exercise rooms, saunas—in short, all the amenities of a private club? It's not only economically feasible, but more important, it will satisfy people.

These graciously planned apartments of tomorrow will make our present imageless structures obsolete, unless they're remodeled to give tenants not just shelter, but shelter plus spacious environment and a way of life.

More important even than spaciously aesthetic environment and special amenities is gracious host-guest management. The best management is a hostlike attitude devoid of commercialization. In a special sense is not the tenant your guest? It's not enough to cater to physical wants. Management must learn to genuinely care for people. That's when a landlord-tenant relationship can be transmuted into a host-guest graciousness that transcends money.

Enlightened management can give people a sense of belonging. It can tactfully plan evenings for the tenant-guests so they become wholesomely involved with one another, whether for an evening of cards, a timely lecture, home movie, or perhaps on-the-house coffee and cookies, several evenings a week.

Leisure can bless and burn. It burns when we don't know what to do with it. It blesses when we do. Enlightened management can creatively direct some of their tenants' leisure by responsible planning. If it is done imaginatively each tenant can have his privacy, yet participate enthusiastically with others if he wants to.

What a far cry this kind of understanding management is from the type which only has an eye for a dollar and the last line of an operating statement. Harsh commercialization leads to irritability and character deterioration, and eventually, in my opinion, to a lower rate of return.

Host-guest management, aside from its spiritual good, conserves real estate values. More than aesthetics and special amenities, as desirable as they are, host-guest management gives real estate men the opportunity to combine idealism with practical business principles.

Downtown malls

Building an occasional new building amidst blight will not rejuvenate a worn out downtown. But a mall covering several blocks will do it because it has dramatic impact. A mall does more than a new building. It separates automobiles from people. It creates a spacious environment. Its effect is visually horizontal rather than remotely vertical. It offers a respite from stop-and-go lights. It slows down the pace of city life by cre-

ating a relaxing atmosphere where people can walk and browse
in leisure.

There is a resistance throughout the country to converting
main downtown streets into malls because store keepers are
leery about having their store fronts face a garden atmosphere.
Though the shopping centers over the country feature display
windows overlooking winding walks and manicured gardens,
the dyed-in-the-wool downtowners, more out of tradition than
logic, have been reluctant to give up the questionable advantage of having cars passing their show windows.

To overcome this resistance I suggest a plan which, with
some variations, can be adapted to most of America's downtowns. Instead of turning the main thoroughfare into a mall,
build the mall at the rear of a row of successful, main street
stores. Property values usually drop sharply in areas adjoining
the main street stores. Most downtowns will have several areas
where such a situation exists. Let me describe a section I
picked in Milwaukee which could be used as a pilot mall.

Between Fourth and Fifth Streets on the south side of Wisconsin Avenue—Milwaukee's number one business street—are
two and a half blocks of aging hotels, an old YMCA building,
several sliver parking lots and single story stores which were
economically marginal. At the southern-most tip of the area
was an old Wells Fargo building that was used for parking
and repairing automobiles. I estimated their value at about
$3,000,000.

Anchored on Fourth Street, on the east border of the mall
area, is a large and thriving department store. And on the west
end, at Fifth Street and Wisconsin Avenue, is Milwaukee's
largest hotel, The Schroeder. As we shall see shortly these were
two good reasons for locating the mall between them.

My plan called for razing the blighted buildings and erecting in their place a concrete slab 17 feet above street level, beginning at the rear of the Wisconsin Avenue stores and covering

the two and a half blocks. It would bridge Michigan Street—which parallels Wisconsin Avenue—and end at the East-West Expressway. This slab, the basis of the mall, could be reached via escalators from Wisconsin Avenue where a twenty foot alley could be vacated by the city and provide an opening to the elevated mall. Underneath the slab would be two tiers of parking for approximately 1,000 cars. There would be four additional entrances to the elevated mall from the parking area.

My plan called for the following developments for the 250 foot by 800 foot raised area. On the perimeter, I would build about 100,000 square feet of store space. In the center of the mall would be a glass domed inner space, about 125 feet wide and 600 feet long, which the stores would face. This inner mall would become the year 'round centerpiece for the project. Exotic plants, grass, trees, shrubbery, statuary, interesting exhibits and winding walks would blend aesthetically to create a world of leisure away from the commotion of Wisconsin Avenue, 17 feet below.

Above the mall and the stores would rise a skyscraper apartment village in the sky, an office building, and a small luxury hotel. The spacious and beautiful mall grounds below would provide the magnet for people to want to be there. It would paradoxically have an air of leisurely excitement.

And now a word about its economic feasibility. Our city makes special concessions to entrepreneurs who create parking for its parking-starved downtown. My plan called for the city to use its power of eminent domain to purchase the land for my estimated $3,000,000, add $1,000,000 for the construction of the parking facility, and float a $4,000,000 municipal bond issue at 3 per cent to be amortized at the rate of $200,000 a year including interest and principal until paid. Since the city had gone into similar financial arrangements in order to expand its parking, this would not be an unreasonable request.

The estimated revenue from the 1,000 parking stalls, backed by the opinions of parking experts, was $200,000 a year. There were three parking generator reasons for this high estimate: the department store, The Schroeder Hotel and the 100,000 square feet of stores on the mall.

I estimated the cost of the mall, its weather-protected amenities over the parking structure, and the 100,000 square feet of store space at $2,000,000. Since this portion of the project would not qualify for special financing I would have to use conventional mortgage methods of amortizing $2,000,000 at 6 per cent in 25 years, or provide for a yearly payment of $155,-000. If I leased the 100,000 square feet of store space at $3 per square foot per year, my $300,000 yearly income would be more than enough to amortize the $2,000,000 loan at $155,000 a year, and pay the estimated $100,000 a year of fixed expenses including real estate taxes, heat, management, etc. This would leave me a cash overage of $45,000 a year. I did not provide for real estate taxes for the $4,000,000 land and parking structure which the city would finance because it does not receive real estate taxes on similarly financed parking structures.

When I informed the owners of the department store of my mall idea they were delighted. They not only agreed to a tentative parking ticket validation plan which would produce $100,000 a year income, but suggested that I connect the mall with the second floor of their department store by bridging over Fourth Street. They even volunteered to lease 30,000 square feet of the stores on the mall. The Schroeder Hotel executives were equally enthusiastic about bridging over Fifth Street to their second floor public area space, and of course, they too showed interest in using my undercover parking for their hotel patrons.

The economic bonanza in the mall plan is the air rights to the four acres of valuable downtown land. Without land cost it would be no problem to mortgage an apartment or office building at close to 100 per cent. The cash overage from each of these buildings could be substantial—perhaps as high as $50,000 a year.

Let's review the advantages of this mall concept.

It does not interfere with store owners who refuse to turn their main street into a mall. It gets it above and away from them.

It creates undercover parking where it's needed—seconds away from the parking stall to hotel, department store, or upper mall area.

It plows under a large area of blight and replaces it with an oasis of beauty where people can shop conveniently and leisurely, away from present downtown noise and congestion.

The bridging over to other buildings can be extended to other streets, thus expanding the concept of above-street shopping to similarly constructed adjoining malls above street level. What's wrong with leaving the noise and parking below and enjoying year 'round weather-protected shopping comfort above? It makes sense. Even more sense than the shopping centers where parking is often blocks away from the stores.

What makes still more sense is its economic feasibility. The elevated mall concept can be built without any great outlay of capital. The logic of the idea is what makes it possible. When you can use land for three purposes—parking, stores and skyscrapers—you have found a formula that lets the economic laws work for you. And when you can have them operate within a plan which creates a new real estate form, providing beauty and function, you have an idea that is ripe for action.

As of this writing the elevated mall idea in Milwaukee has been set in motion. A similar plan can be devised with local improvisation in any downtown American city. It doesn't take money to give it viability. It takes explaining, persuasion and perseverance. And above all, an inspirational dedication that you are pioneering the real estate of tomorrow.

Recreation of tomorrow

Leisure adds meaning to living if it helps to give us a sense of purpose through music, literature, theology, or art. The shrinking work week gives us time not only to appreciate culture, but to participate in it actively.

However, too much culture is like too much dessert. For a balanced leisure life it is necessary to participate in recreational activity, preferably as doers rather than viewers. Watching football, baseball and basketball games is not quite as good as golfing, fishing or boating. Spectator sports actively involve the few, while the many look on. Recreation should be the other way around. We need more participative recreation for two good reasons—to involve more people and to start new industries.

OLD MCDONALD'S LITTLE FARM

I own an eighty-acre farm twenty-five miles from Milwaukee. It's heavily wooded. A stream meanders through its rolling hills and winding country trails.

Every year I invite the tenants of my office building and their families to spend a few hours of their leisure on my farm. On a perfect July summer day one of my advertising executive tenants and I took a leisurely hike on my farm when it was at its loveliest.

"George," he said, "wouldn't it be wonderful if city children could be exposed to the beauties of a farm like this?" Then he stopped suddenly in his tracks, and said, "Why not? George, I've got an idea!"

His idea is now a reality. He bought a 120-acre farm a few miles from mine, easily reached by automobile from Milwaukee, and created a farm wonderland. He stocked it with cows, horses, pigs, sheep, chickens, geese and ducks. He didn't stop there. He caged the less domesticated rabbits, racoons, foxes, coyotes and pheasants, and distributed them throughout the woods and fields of the farm.

He launched a television, radio and newspaper campaign slanted to children, urging them to ask their parents to take them to Old McDonald's Little Farm. The result was not only a commercial success, it showed how hungry children were for sweet country air, the sight of woods and fields, and farm animals. Charging 50 cents admission for children and 75 cents for adults, my tenant friend grossed $10,000 a week.

He created side-line attractions. He charged 15 cents for a cup of food which the children bought to feed the animals. There are hay rides, pony rides, and picnicking in the woods. There is a snack bar featuring Old McDonald's Little Farm's own products, such as fresh buttermilk, honey in the comb, berries and farm-baked fresh bread and cookies. A large garden area was set aside and subdivided into miniature beds, where for a nominal one dollar a summer a child could have his own garden area to grow his favorite plants and vegetables. In this way my friend hoped to have steady child patrons coming to tend their gardens, feed the animals, and spend many days on the farm.

His future plans call for building an artificial lake which he will stock with fish. He'll charge the children ten cents for every fish they catch. His aim is to load the farm with many attractions at low prices.

The tens of thousands of children who were taken to Old McDonald's Little Farm kept urging their parents to take them there again and again. The farm was meeting a need. The children were having wholesome fun in a wholesome atmosphere, and it was helping to bring the parents and children closer together.

Every large city in America could support several of these farms on its outskirts. It makes sense commercially, but more important, it offers city youngsters a taste of farm life which they could otherwise only get vicariously through reading, picture books, or seeing it from a fast moving car.

LIGHTED GOLF COURSES

Golf has been mainly a game for the classes. By lighting up golf courses for night play, it could become large-scale recreation for the masses. It has happened in baseball, it is happening in football, and it could happen in golf. Golf's advantage over baseball and football is that it is a participative activity.

The average white and blue collar worker can only be a weekend golfer, and if he has chores to do around the house, those weekends can become scarce. With night golf, the office or factory worker can get home, wash up, have his meal and play a round before bedtime. For the same reason that there is greater attendance of night games than day games, there would be more play on golf courses at night than during the day.

It costs about $200,000 to light up a typical regulation 18 hole golf course for night play. Because the investment in building a golf course is so large, only a few have been built as business enterprises. The great majority of golf courses are either private country clubs or municipally owned. However, well conceived golf courses upon which people could play day and night could easily become sound business propositions. It could double or triple the 6,000,000 people who play golf today.

Golf need not remain mainly the exclusive game of country club members. It's too wonderful a game to be enjoyed by the few. Night golf, promoted on the basis of private or public enterprise, can wholesomely engage more of our leisure hours, increase production in the golf industry, and make millions more physically fit.

LEISURE CLUBS

On one of my trips through Wisconsin, I was shown a Veterans of Foreign Wars clubhouse in Oshkosh on two acres of land with riparian rights on Lake Winnebago. The property was for sale but no one seemed to know what to do with it. The broker who showed it to me asked, "What would you do with it? The veterans no longer need it, and I can't seem to find anyone who does. Got any ideas?"

"Yes," I said, "I've got an idea, but it'll take a lot of work." I was thinking about channeling leisure through new real estate forms. I suggested the following plan:

"Put together a syndicate of five well-known people in Oshkosh and have each of them invest $20,000, form a corporation, and capitalize it for $100,000. Purchase the property for the asking price of $100,000, which in my estimation is a bargain. Remodel and upgrade the clubhouse so it includes a sauna, restaurant, large meeting room, library and other areas to house interest in arts, crafts, music, and such activities. Build two tennis courts, four bowling alleys, a swimming pool, a marina dock, a few shuffleboard courts and a putting green. I would estimate the cost of all these at about $150,000. I suggest you arrange for a first mortgage of $150,000 to be amortized over twenty-five years.

"After you describe this improvement program to your five syndicators you're ready to explain the next step—its economic feasibility. First you must show them how they can get their money back and a profit. By selling 250 family memberships at $100 a year the syndicators would get their investment returned in four years. The corporation by-laws could provide that the original investors are to receive another $100,000 in profit by continuing to charge the $100 yearly fees for another four years, and then discontinue them. This need not be the only plan. There could be variations of it.

"Be sure to point out to the investors that they are doing more than making a profit—they are helping to create a recreational facility which will build their community. And to assure them that they will make their profit, point out that the yearly interest and amortization on the $150,000 loan will be only $11,500. A modest profit from membership bowling, restaurant, marina, and perhaps nominal fees from the tennis courts and the swimming pool would be enough to pay off the low yearly payment on the mortgage. Most of the personnel to run the leisure club could be recruited from among the members, some on a part time and some on a full time basis. Since this facility would cater to the lower middle class income group, the appointments and services need not be extravagant so that the operational budget would not have to depend upon the $100 yearly membership fees. They could be safely set aside for the investors until they received their original investment plus the agreed-upon profit."

I told the broker that if he thought through my suggestions and prepared sketches and a brochure spelling out its economic feasibility, he could create a beehive of wholesome activity on the grounds that now stand empty and forlorn. By putting this problem property to its highest and best use, the broker would earn a commission, 250 families would be grateful for the new ways to spend their leisure, the community of Oshkosh would gain generally and five investors would profit specifically.

Every city in America from 50,000 and up would become a better community if one or more of the leisure clubs I have described could be sensibly promoted. And the real estate men of America ought to be the ones to spark their development.

OVERNIGHT HOSTELS

The one to two hundred yard strips of land adjoining both sides of our superhighways which I suggested earlier should be set aside for horseback riding, hiking, bicycle, and horse and buggy trails could, if imaginatively promoted, become a new form of recreation involving millions of people. And the idea could create a new industry.

As real estate professionals, we would be making an important contribution to the American people if we could provide the physical environment to slow down our feverish pace of living. We could do it by beautifying the paths and trails along the superhighways and building overnight hostels, restaurants and other special stop-over points of interest to encourage and make pleasant traveling by horse and buggy, bicycles and horses. And these scenic trails could be a paradise for hikers. Would not spending several weeks traveling more primitively be as satisfying as racing 500 miles a day to get to places faster and further away? Is the destination at the end of a 3,000 mile trip so different from that at the end of a leisurely 300 mile journey? Is not the means as important as the end? I am not suggesting that we give up the faster mode of travel. I am suggesting that we can have both.

Those who nostalgically remember or read about the good old days when life was more leisurely, can have it, if we create the physical environment to wean people away from the ever-increasing speed, and give them an opportunity to choose less hectic ways to live and travel.

What a wholesome and worthwhile project for men of imagination to tackle—to bring back the leisure of bygone days, give new life to an old industry, and most important, through the creation of a new physical environment, change the traveling habits of people from speed to sense!

8.

Pitfall Investments– Stay Away

It's easy to create real estate equities if you have imagination, and just as easy to lose them if you don't. Real estate equities are like quicksilver—now you have them, and now you don't. The one sure way to stabilize value is to nail it down with a long term lease guaranteed by a multibillion dollar corporation. But unfortunately this can be done only on rare occasions.

In recent years, due to the dynamic changes taking place in the real estate market, values have become highly changeable. In many instances they have skyrocketed in one area and plummeted in another. Land values in Milwaukee's downtown, for instance, have dropped in many cases to one-half, while at the same time land values in a suburban neighborhood shopping center have increased tenfold.

Only the exceedingly alert who are sensitive to trends know when to buy, when to sell, when to build and when to hold on to their investments. It takes facts and intuition to form a composite judgment from such variables as a neighborhood trend, the city's economic health and the general state of the national economy. Each has a bearing on the value of a specific piece of real estate.

In addition to neighborhood, community and national trends, there is the variable factor of human nature. I know a half dozen real estate men who have gone to the wall because they became so intoxicated with their initial successes that they lost touch with reality, and began dreaming of the applause they would receive if they could pyramid their equities into a real estate fortune.

Many capable men, mesmerized by the siren song of success, lose sight of the dynamic law of change, and continue to make decisions as though change didn't exist. They get sucked in by real estate undertows.

The following examples spotlight some of the treacherous currents which can capsize anyone who is not alert to real estate trends, and to the pitfalls in his own human nature.

Loft building: Five years of work for nothing

If you let success blind you, you'll grope in a fog. I did, for five years.

A growing ice cream manufacturing company sold its aging and obsolete 40,000 square foot, five story, mill constructed building and its equally obsolete adjoining 75,000 square foot, five story garage for $125,000 to a meat dealer. It timed the sale during a year when it was in a high income bracket so as to minimize its loss.

The meat dealer tried to lease these buildings without success. He was a successful purveyor of meat, but as is often the case, one can be a big gun in his own business, and a pop gun in another. He was stuck with two white elephants. They remained vacant for a year.

Flushed with several recent successes I was an easy mark for this deal. Without carefully examining the trends in the neighborhood and not perceiving the beginning of an industrial exodus from the inner core area to the outskirts, I signed a ninety-nine year lease for both buildings at $15,000 a year.

I took one precaution which saved me. I formed a shell corporation to assume the lease, thus limiting my personal liability.

Remodeling the 40,000 square foot ice cream manufacturing building was a nightmare. To save my sanity I called it a challenge.

It took a week to melt the ice in the walls of the refrigerated area. It had been in this frozen state for twenty years. It seemed as if the ice were holding up the building. After tearing out miles of ammonia-carrying copper pipes, shoring up the sagging floors with steel beams, and rewiring the maze of dead and loose wires, I leased the first floor to a wholesale druggist, and the four floors above to an instrument-making company. With a stroke of luck, I rented the 75,000 square foot garage building to American Motors Corp. for storage. The annual rent from the two buildings was $65,000. I spent $100,000 for remodeling. For five years I cleared $20,000 annually.

Then, American Motors moved out. I tried in vain to find a new tenant. What I hadn't realized was that the movement from the inner downtown area to the outskirts had now become a stampede. With the garage building vacant, my $20,000 a year profit became a $15,000 a year loss.

I called the lessor and said: "We're in trouble."

"What do you mean, *we're* in trouble" he said, good-naturedly. "*You're* in trouble!"

"No," I said, "*we're* in trouble because I'm ready to give the building back to you."

I pointed out to him that I had no personal liability on the ninety-nine year lease. I told him, however, that I would do everything I could to avert the collapse of the corporation. He said he would cooperate, if I came up with an answer that made economic sense to him and to me. I couldn't ask for more.

I began looking for a plan that would get us both out from

under a losing proposition. Someone called my attention to a products display studio which had outgrown its old dilapidated building. When I asked the president if he would be interested in my 75,000 square foot garage building, he said, yes, providing I took his building in trade.

We agreed that he would pay $125,000 for the garage building and that I would allow him $60,000 for his antiquated studio building. It was a ridiculously one-sided deal, but I had no choice—I had to make a move.

I called my lessor and gave him the following proposition:

I told him that for and in consideration of dissolving the corporation which signed the ninety-nine year lease, I would be willing to pay him $165,000 in cash for the fee in his two buildings. I disclosed the offer I received from the owner of the products display studio.

Although the meat dealer, I'm sure, would have preferred to continue getting $15,000 a year for the next ninety-three years, he realized it was not possible, and he agreed to accept my offer.

I now owned the 40,000 square foot ice cream plant building and a dilapidated old studio for $100,000. I paid $165,000 to the meat packer and received $65,000 in cash when I traded with the studio owner. To make matters worse, I received an order from the city that the foundation of the old ice cream plant was sinking dangerously, and that it needed shoring up in a hurry. I put $25,000 into the ground that did not add a jot of value to the building. The two buildings now cost me $125,000.

My main problem was to get rid of the vacant studio building. With a little luck and hard work, and I discovered the harder I worked the luckier I got, I interested a wholesale plumbing wares firm in the neighborhood in the vacant studio building for parking, and sold it for $50,000. I sold the ice cream building for $75,000 several months later.

What a lot of sound and fury I stirred up which came to nothing when my accountant showed me the figures. My five years of effort in risking, remodeling, leasing, selling, and trading showed a several thousand dollar loss. Only my persevering maneuvering prevented the deal from eroding into a serious loss.

But looking at this deal from another angle, I gained a valuable lesson. I turned down several similar propositions which could have gotten me into deep financial trouble. I learned several hard facts which only experience could have taught me.

The rewarding aspect of this involved deal was that I did not allow my corporation to default on the ninety-nine year lease. Though I was not legally liable, I would have lost an intangible, had I collapsed my corporation, and defaulted. That precious intangible is living up to one's obligation. The meat packer is still my good friend, and that's a valuable asset.

Commercial downtown building: My foolish offer is saved by a more foolish refusal

The time was ripe in 1952, I thought, to pioneer the development of modernized downtown office space. I began to look for an older building that could be remodeled.

My search stopped with the Security Building, an 80,000 square foot, eight story building on North Second Street and West Wisconsin Avenue. It had a ready-to-wear store on the ground floor, and seven floors of office space, renting from 50 cents to $1.50 a square foot per year. I was dealing with the owners of a leasehold interest which had forty years to go at $30,000 a year. What I didn't realize at the time was that the exodus for office space away from downtown had already begun.

Blinded by an ideal location and my ambition to own downtown property, I offered $800,000 for the leasehold rights of

the Security Building. It was one of the most foolish offers I
had made in my real estate career. My good fortune was that
the owners were more foolish in refusing it.

In 1960, the leasehold was sold for $125,000, and within a
year the buyer lost it on foreclosure. The erosion of value in
the Security Building during the 1950's symbolized the real
estate history of many old downtown commercial buildings
in America. The main reasons which caused values to fall were
the moving of offices to the outskirts, the encroachments on
downtown retail volume by shopping centers, and the maintenance of unrealistically high downtown real estate taxes.

The Security Building is now owned by the estate whose
ancestors made the original lease. Even during the depression
the price of the building did not erode down to the fee interest. In 1964, the bedraggled building stood as a symbol
of where our downtowns were heading. The same kind of a
dynamic idea that is needed to put the Security Building in
the black is needed to revive downtowns in general. The usual
ideas will not do.

The land is too expensive for razing the Security Building,
and putting up a single story retail outlet. The location is not
good for an office building because it is landlocked by expensive property on all sides, and therefore the cost would be
prohibitive to provide close-in parking. Also, there are several
hundred thousand square feet of new office space which the
market has yet to digest. Nor is the land suitable for a hotel
or an apartment building.

When answers will be more readily found for specific parcels of downtown property, it will become easier to find an
answer for the overall downtown area. Until those specific and
general answers are found, downtown property will remain
a hazardous investment, even for the professional real estate
man. My advice to unsophisticated investors is to stay away
from downtown real estate until definite trends develop.

Apartment building: Stripped down luxury reveals the builders' motives

The first allegiance of entrepreneurs should be to develop their own community. Before looking for greener pastures they should meet the local needs. Their community feeds them, and they should in turn contribute to their community. It's common sense and it makes economic sense as well.

Several Chicago real estate men thought they knew more about the Milwaukee apartment market than the local people. They bought a sliver of land overlooking Lake Michigan, built fifty-seven apartments, and promoted it as a luxury project.

It failed for several reasons. The owners attempted to create a luxury image on postage-stamp land. They offered obviously stripped down luxury which revealed the builders' motives, and left them just as bare. The apartments were too high priced for the middle income group, and not good enough for those who were looking for genuine luxury. The immediately surrounding area had several old, ill kept buildings which cast their depreciating shadows, and dulled the glitter of the new apartments.

Two years after the pseudo-luxury building went up, only seventeen apartments were rented. Not only had the owners' equity disappeared, but the $900,000 first mortgage was in jeopardy. This is what can happen when the wrong people put a wrong project in a wrong location.

The building has no amenities to give it a character image for the long pull investment. By making cut rate concessions the building may be filled, but it will always be a struggle to hold the tenants. Neither the owners nor the financiers were aware what luxury apartments of the future should be like. Apparently they kept their eyes too close to economics, and didn't see where they missed on satisfying people.

It is economically imprudent to strip a long term investment for short term goals. Sooner or later an entrepreneur will short change himself if he short changes an investment in lot size, location, or amenities. Plan and give in full measure, and it will be returned to you in kind, and for a long time.

High priced land: Don't let ambition fool you

For several years I had my eye on a 250 by 250 foot block of land which I thought was an ideal site for two hundred semi-luxury apartments. These, I figured, could rent for $175 per month for a one-bedroom unit, $250 for a two-bedroom unit, and $300 for a three-bedroom unit.

It had an unusual location. To the east was a city park beyond which was a high bluff plunging into Lake Michigan. To the south was a spacious two lane boulevard with wide beds of flowers separating the traffic lanes. To the north was an attractive new hotel, and to the west, an older area which was slated for demolition, and urban renewal.

On this spacious acre and a half of land, I planned my 200 unit high rise apartment building with its own parklike environment.

I was in the process of assembling the land from its several owners for about $500,000. This would come to $2,500 per unit in my building. I was on the verge of sewing it up when a group of out-of-town syndicators got wind of it, and hurriedly (too hurriedly, they found out to their regret) bought it for $850,000. I was both disappointed and surprised, disappointed that I did not get the land, and surprised that they paid such a high price for it.

I believe they paid too much for the land because they figured out an easy way to acquire it. They leased the north half of it from the owner for $25,000 a year on a fifty year lease, thus placing a $500,000 value on it. They paid $350,000 to the several owners for the south half, and obtained a $250,000 short-term mortgage, so that they controlled the entire parcel for $100,000. I met one of the syndicators who was involved in the deal, and asked him what was planned for the site. He told me they were going to build 350 apartments in order to bring down the ratio of land cost to apartment unit.

I told him their plans were not realistic. It's one thing for a city like Chicago to fill 350 apartments in one building, it's another in a city the size of Milwaukee. To apply the same standards to a 750,000 population city that makes sense in a 5,000,000 population metropolis can be economically misleading.

They were caught in a dilemma. If they built fewer apartments, like the 200 I planned, their land cost per unit would be abnormally high.

For two years they held on to the land, paying $25,000 a year on half of it, and interest on the $250,000 mortgage. Too much ambition, too little regard for facts, and easy financing were the siren chorus that caused them to overpay for the land. To make the project feasible they either had to come up with more cash or abandon it. They let it go.

Many such failures result from inordinate ambition, the incubator for faulty reasoning. When runaway ambition strikes it can cut down the most sophisticated and knowledgeable. It has no respect for success. I have known men who have climbed to real estate prominence and suddenly slipped into failure and bankruptcy. Their downfall was unbridled ambition. It's a disease which blurs the vision and fogs reason. Watch out for it. It's deadly.

Flats and rooming houses: They may bring high returns—but for how long?

Tens of thousands of wage earners like to augment their incomes by investing their small savings in low priced investment real estate such as duplexes and rooming houses. Since they do not have much money to invest, they don't mind buying trouble property as long as they bring a high rate of return. Most of them expect at least 20 per cent return on their investment. Only marginal properties offer such a high return. However, the pitfall in this investment philosophy is that the high return usually lasts only a short time. The dynamics of change hits the marginal investment more often and with greater impact than the more conventional stable investments.

The paralysis of blight which changes neighborhood characteristics as it creeps along, and the general rise in standards of living which prompts families to move, have combined to cause good neighborhoods to become fair, fair neighborhoods to become marginal, and marginal neighborhoods to become poor.

Several of my salesmen bought high-yield investment property in good and fair neighborhoods in the middle 1950's only to see them dwindle to no yield at all in the early 1960's. Imperceptibly, almost in front of their noses, changes were occurring which pushed the good and fair neighborhoods into marginal and poor ones. The virus of blight attacked dozens of square blocks of properties. Tenants with rising standards of living, who had pride in well maintained properties, left the deteriorating neighborhoods for better ones. A vicious circle began. Those who were left behind cared less for cleanliness and upkeep than those who left, thus accelerating the rate of blight. The flight from blight by those who got better paying jobs became a stampede. "For Rent" signs plastered the blighted areas, while at the same time there was a shortage of housing at fair rentals in better neighborhoods.

One type of problem brings on new problems. The City Inspection Department clamped down on owners to fix up their blighted real estate or raze it. In many instances, the cost of remodeling was so prohibitive, and the prospect of renting to responsible tenants so poor, that the owners threw in the sponge, and let their properties be foreclosed. Some of my salesmen along with thousands of other small investors were trapped in this avalanche of real estate deterioration.

Our company did not come out unscathed either. In the process of trading properties, we acquired an inventory of rooming houses, duplexes, and cottages in these fast-changing neighborhoods. Maintenance problems with marginal tenants in poor neighborhoods become mountainous. We were forced to raze about a dozen properties because they were beyond repair. The problem we faced, however, was that our company signed the mortgages on these properties so that we not only lost our equities but had to pay up the balances on the mortgages as well.

By the middle 1960's we had 150 tenants in the blighted areas. In some instances we held the blight at bay, in others we repaired to satisfy the City Inspection Department, and in still others we remodeled in order to attract better tenants. From 1955 to 1965, we not only failed to realize a 20 per cent return, but we showed substantial losses. The high cost of management and maintenance, and loss of rentals, have kept us in the red during all the time we owned the marginal properties in the poor neighborhoods. Our only help came when we were able to sell some of the parcels to the city to make way for expressways and urban renewal.

Many small investors lost their meager savings in this segment of the real estate market. This threat of dynamic change is hanging over every American city. It would behoove every small investor to weigh carefully the minuses and pluses of a neighborhood before he lays his hard earned money on the line. What looks like a good investment today can become a fair one two years from now, and a poor one five years hence. A small entrepreneur can become a poor entrepreneur almost overnight. Big returns quickly become no returns.

Stay away from these pitfall investments unless you can peer into a neighborhood's future and realistically and intuitively see what will happen to it in two, three, five, or ten years. If you don't know, stay away.

Co-operative apartment building: Owner and city hurt each other

This is the story of how a city's unrealistic zoning restrictions veered a well planned co-operative apartment project into a wrong location, and failure. Milwaukee has many grand old homes overlooking Lake Michigan. But many of them are old and too large to meet today's needs. Unfortunately, however, whenever an entrepreneur tries to rezone the lake bluff area for apartments, the old-time residents who control these sites pounce on the developer with such vehement objection that the city refuses to change the zoning code. Large cities which have had success with luxury co-operatives have gone to bat for the developers, and re-zoned attractive areas to match the environment of the home dwellers who wanted to move into luxury apartments.

A successful Milwaukee builder, anticipating the pent up demand for co-operative luxury apartments, set out to fill the need in spite of the city's unenlightened zoning policy. Unable to find a spacious lot in an attractive area to insure the success of his project, he made the mistake of building eighty-two co-operative luxury apartments on Prospect Avenue, an artery of northbound traffic. And to compound his mistake he built them on a sliver of a lot, only 100 feet wide by 200 feet deep. Although the land was on the lake side of Prospect Avenue, the blight of mixed zoning which allowed rooming houses, public institutions and nursing homes in its immediate vicinity neutralized the lake view advantage. He reached out desperately for the luxury apartment buyers but they were not desperate enough to buy—not in a second rate location.

I saw the brochure on the co-operative venture and, based

on a quick calculation, I saw a half a million dollar profit to
the owner if he had been able to sell the apartments on the
basis of an average of $40,000 for a 2000 square foot apart-
ment. He could have done it on Wahl Avenue or Lake Drive
if the city had helped him re-zone these sites for luxury apartments. They were natural sites. Prospect Avenue was unnatural.

Although the building was well constructed and the apartments well designed, the project failed. The owner did not
make the half million dollars. After two years of hard selling
only forty of eighty-two apartments were sold at close to the
asking price. To sell the rest the developer had to pay inflated
prices for the homes which the buyers "traded" for apartments. It was four years before the last apartment was sold.
The ill starred venture was a failure from the standpoint of
both the developer and those who bought the apartments.
Many of the buyers were unhappy with their new environment—it was a far cry from what they had left. The developer
was unhappy, too. Instead of making a half million dollars, he
lost money and endured four years of frustration.

Luxury apartment prospects come from expensive homes,
and want a residential environment similar to the ones they
had enjoyed.

The Milwaukee co-operative luxury apartment failure illustrates that even if there is a pressing demand for such housing,
if the need is not met scientifically—that is, custom built to the
local habits and mores of the people—it has a better chance of
failing than succeeding.

Small office buildings: The shorter the leases the longer the gamble

The 1950's witnessed a migration of office space users from
downtown to the outskirts. To take advantage of this trend,
enterprisers built small office buildings on heavily trafficked

streets several miles from downtown. Neighborhood doctors, lawyers, insurance companies and manufacturer's agents were typical tenants for these buildings. Several hundred thousand square feet of these miniature office buildings sprang up in Milwaukee on Capital Drive and Fond du Lac Avenue. These streets are typical of those that have enticed office tenants from downtown in every large American city.

The average small office building has attention-arresting architectural lines, ample adjoining parking and is fully air conditioned. The builders, at least those in Milwaukee, have managed to "mortgage out" these ventures from 80 to 100 per cent.

Small office buildings are not good long-term investments. Since the typical leases are from one to five years, the owner of such a building is constantly faced with the threat of a 20 to 30 per cent vacancy any time one or more of the tenants decides to move. And since cash overage (that is, money left after fixed expenses and interest and principal payments are deducted from gross income) is usually figured on the basis of 100 per cent occupancy, there is little cash left in a highly mortgaged building if it is not 100 per cent occupied. A 10 to 20 per cent vacancy not only wipes out what cash there is left, but usually means "taking money from home."

While small office buildings are dazzlingly new, they are attractive. But in five or ten years, many lose their character. A small building becomes shabby looking because it cannot afford an on-site manager and on-the-premises maintenance man which downtown office buildings have. Another drawback is that they are usually too far removed from the secretarial and stenographic labor market. And, helped by expressways and urban renewal, some downtowns are beginning to make comebacks, and some tenants who left for the outskirts are returning.

Unless you can buy a small office building which has a 15

per cent return on your equity investment, and unless you have many business friends and know a good many professional people, so that in case of a vacancy you have a good chance to lease it to them, don't invest in a small office building. By all means, don't fall for the selling argument, "you may not receive a return on your investment now, but when you pay off the mortgage from the income you'll own it free and clear." This is a specious argument. You should expect a return on your investment now, not fifteen, twenty, or twenty-five years from now. The chances are the building you buy now will have little residual value in the future.

Four-families: Unique architecture, unusual location and live-in owner are needed to make it successful

A few rungs higher on the investment ladder than the inner core duplexes and rooming houses are the new four-family apartment buildings which cater to the small investor. The city of Milwaukee has been flooded with them. Amateur builders can buy a lot for $10,000, build a four family flat for about $36,000, including land, and "mortgage out" at $35,000. Volume builders of four-families not only "mortgaged out" 100 per cent, but in some instances, they had money left over.

The typical dwelling unit in such a flat has about 900 square feet consisting of a small living room, dinette, kitchen, two bedrooms and a bath. The average yearly operating expense for the four units, including taxes, insurance, maintenance, and interest and principal amortization on a $35,000 mortgage, is about $4,500. The average rent per apartment is $95 a month, or $4,560 a year for the four units. One vacancy drags the occupancy rate down to 75 per cent, and becomes a loss of over a thousand dollars a year.

Most four-families are built without the aid of an architect, and they show it. They are characterless. Few give a feeling of uniqueness. We have several projects where you can see row upon row of four-families as far as the eye can reach, and although the builders had made a weak attempt at variation, the result was barren and barracklike. Each free standing building is no different from the next, and each apartment looks as if it came out of the same cookie cutter. Such projects are the tenements of the future.

Conclusive evidence that four-family flats are not good investments is the fact that during the early sixties when business was booming and employment was at an all time high in Milwaukee, hundreds of these were being foreclosed. Builders who did not want their names recorded in the foreclosure statistics offered $500 per building to any responsible businessman who was willing to assume its outstanding mortgage—that's how bad the four-family apartment market became as a result of overbuilding, lack of architectural character and fierce competition for tenants. Price wars developed in which a $10 cut in rent caused hundreds of families to shift from one nondescript building to another, and from one dreary project to another equally as drab.

Unless a four-family apartment building has unique architecture, unusual location and an owner who will live on the premises to supervise it, a four-family, a six-, or even an eight-family is not a good long-term real estate investment.

A landlocked office building: If experts get hurt, so can you

The up and down history of the Empire Building in Milwaukee underscores the uncertainty and danger of dealing in landlocked downtown office buildings.

In the mid-1950's a nationally known syndicator must have merely slowed down his airplane to check the Empire before he bought it for a reported $1,750,000. It is located on one of the key downtown corners. This is what must have mesmerized him. But apparently this real estate tycoon did not know the local Milwaukee conditions. The building had no parking, with no chance to get any, because the surrounding property was too high priced. And he didn't have time to analyze the office demand trend away from downtown, which started as a trickle in the early 1950's, and by the time of his purchase had become a stream. The tenants in the Empire were leading the parade to the outskirts.

Until World War II, the Empire was one of the leading office buildings in the city. The sophisticated syndicator must have been more impressed with its record than concerned with its future. After two years of ownership, the occupancy rate dropped to 70 per cent. The Eastern syndicator must have taken a half-million dollar loss, and sold it to an experienced Chicago syndicator for about $1,250,000.

The Midwesterner did not fare any better. In fact, he did worse. His occupancy dropped to 50 per cent. I remember how frantic he was when he came to my office one day and said:

"George, what's wrong with your city? I've got prime space and nobody wants it. The local manager I've hired can't seem to find tenants, and I can't afford to spend too much time here myself. What do you suggest? I've got half a million dollars in this deal, and I can't see daylight until I get eighty per cent occupancy."

"I'm afraid you've misjudged Milwaukee, as your predecessor did," I said. "You have a second rate, landlocked building that has enjoyed years of downtown office supremacy, and is now at the end of its cycle. Unless you can get a top manager who is an expert in getting new tenants, and unless you're willing to back him with several hundred thousand dollars in remodeling, you're going to have an uphill battle with little chance of winning it."

He wasn't able to find expert management, and he was wary

about adding more to his original $500,000 investment. Within several years he lost the building and his $500,000 investment.

A local entrepreneur bought it for $750,000. He made a success of it because he bought it at a bargain, he gave it his personal attention, he spent several hundred thousand dollars in upgrading it, and sold custom built, fully air conditioned office space at the extremely attractive price of $2.75 per square foot per year. He squeezed a million dollars worth of "water" out of the deal—that helped most of all.

Old downtown office buildings are pitfall investments. What has happened to the Empire has happened to other buildings in other cities.

Its checkered experience should be a red flag to anyone who is contemplating purchasing downtown property. If experts get hurt, so can you.

9.

The Leverage Law
of Investment Real Estate

Several decades ago investment yield in real estate was usually described in terms of percentage yield based on free and clear property. Long term amortized mortgages were practically unknown. Straight mortgage financing was the prevailing lending method in those days. The borrower would pay interest until the mortgage became due at a pre-arranged date, usually three to five years. Those who are over fifty years of age will recall that many suspense stories of the silent movies were based on a plot ,where the "good guy" found a way to pay off the mortgage in the nick of time to prevent the "bad guy" from acquiring his girl's homestead.

It would be difficult to concoct a similar plot today. Most of our homes are heavily mortgaged for twenty to thirty years. A free and clear property is a rarity.

The amortized mortgage which replaced the straight mortgage was a boon to the real estate industry. It helped create billions of dollars in new real estate wealth. Amortizing a mortgage over several decades protected the home owner from the sudden crisis of straight mortgage financing, and placed an invaluable financial tool in the hands of the imaginative entrepreneur. The amortized mortgage became a more sophis-

169

ticated financing technique when the Federal Housing Administration, and later private companies, insured the repayment of mortgage loans.

Using the established principle of stretched-out mortgage amortization as the basic idea, the astute real estate investors refined it into what I would like to call the Leverage Law of Investment Real Estate. Its implications are immense for those who understand it, and know how to use it.

The leverage idea began developing in the late 1950's and has grown into an extraordinary effective financial tool in the 1960's. It has made millionaires of those who put it to use. I know several of them.

Stated succinctly, the leverage law means controlling the most real estate with the least money. It means getting the highest cash flow—the money left after all fixed expenses and interest and principal amortization are deducted from gross income—with the least amount of invested capital. The leverage principle works at its finest when there is cash flow without equity investment. That could be called leveraging to infinity.

Examples of leverage

Let's assume a man has $100,000 in cash to invest. Those who are sold on using leverage would consider him unsophisticated if he invested it all in a twelve-family apartment building, and paid for it in cash. Such an investor has no leverage whatsoever. Let's further assume that the apartment building nets $8,000 a year, or an 8 per cent return on the $100,000.

The leverage-minded investor would build a million dollar apartment building, using his $100,000 as seed capital. If he were successful in obtaining a thirty year amortized loan, it is conceivable that after all fixed expenses and interest and principal amortization, the building could generate a cash flow of $15,000 a year. The owner of the $100,000 would then be earning 15% on his equity money, in addition to the amount he would be amortizing yearly on his $900,000 mortgage. On the basis of a thirty year mortgage, the investor would be paying off an average of $30,000 a year on the principal, which when added to the $15,000 cash flow overage, would give him $45,000, or 45 per cent return on his original $100,000 investment. As an additional bonanza, the $15,000 a year cash flow can be tax sheltered, at least for about the first seven years, by taking accelerated depreciation.

Contrast this 45 per cent return with the 8 per cent yield to the investor who bought the twelve-family apartment building for $100,000, and you have a dramatized version of the difference between the conservative free and clear investment philosophy, and the new high voltage leverage concept.

What is applicable to high priced real estate holds for a duplex or a four-family. Let's assume that a duplex can be built for $25,000. It's not to difficult to obtain a 90 per cent or $22,500 mortgage. The owner would thus control $25,000 worth of real estate with his $2,500 down payment. The payments on his $22,500 mortgage on a thirty year basis at 6 per cent are $1,620 a year, to which should be added an estimated $750 for taxes and $380 for miscellaneous, bringing the total payments to $2,750 a year. The owner's return on his $2,250 investment would then be the difference between the $3,000 a year projected income and the $2,750 a year payout, or a cash flow of $250 a year. The owner would thus receive a 10% cash flow return on his $2,500 investment, plus an average yearly $750 principal amortization over the life of the thirty year mortgage, for a total of $1,000 a year, or 40% return on $2,500.

Now what happens if the same owner pays $25,000 cash for the duplex. The taxes are $750 and miscellaneous $380, making a total yearly fixed expense of $1,130, which, subtracted from

$3,000 a year rent, leaves a net profit of $1,870 on a $25,000 investment, or a net return of slightly above 7 per cent.

Obviously, paying $2,500 down, and getting a return of 40 per cent by using the leverage principle, is far more financially rewarding than the 7 per cent net return on the basis of paying $25,000 cash for the duplex.

Using leverage to raise the price of an office building

A certain office building grossed $600,000 a year income. It had a $2,500,000 mortgage balance from an original $2,-800,000 loan based on a twenty-five year amortization with interest at 5 per cent. The interest and principal amortization was $200,000 a year, and the fixed expenses $270,000, leaving a cash flow of approximately $130,000 a year. When the building was put on the market, the best offer the owner was able to get was $3,800,000, based on a cash flow of $130,000 capitalized at 10 per cent. The owner of the building could see while he was negotiating that the investors were more interested in the 10 per cent return of cash flow than in the number of years left on the payment of the mortgage.

The owner offered to pay his building and loan association 5¼ per cent interest, ¼ per cent more than he had been paying, if it would recast the $2,500,000 mortgage balance into a new thirty year amortized mortgage. The lending institution agreed. It amounted to an increase of $6,250 in interest the first year.

The yearly interest and principal payment on the old mortgage was $200,000, and the new recast thirty year amortization payment was $170,000 a year. Thus it increased the cash flow from $130,000 to $160,000 a year without changing the amount of the $2,500,000 mortgage. However, it increased the price of the building by $300,000 because when the owner again put it on the market he had no difficulty getting $4,-

100,000. Applying the leverage principle made the difference. By increasing the cash flow $30,000 a year, the owner capitalized $160,000 at 10 per cent, instead of the previous $130,000 at 10 per cent, and asked and got $1,600,000 above the $2,500,000 mortgage, bettering the previous offer of $1,300,000 above the same mortgage.

I am very familiar with this transaction because this is exactly what happened when I applied the leverage principle, and increased the price of the Bockl Building by $300,000 when I sold it.

Using leverage to create cash flow with no investment

A friend of mine bought 200 garden apartments for $2,350,000, subject to a $2,000,000 mortgage. The cash flow was only $25,000 a year, certainly not enough for a $350,000 cash investment. Many prospects turned it down. Why did my friend buy it? Because he was well versed in the art of leveraging.

My professional investor friend bought the garden apartments not on the strength of the cash flow, since it was barely over 7 per cent, and he rarely bought unless he leveraged 12 per cent, but because he knew he could reconstruct the $2,000,000 mortgage.

Within several months after he bought the apartments, I saw in the vital statistics bulletin what my friend was up to. He obtained a new thirty year $2,350,000 mortgage, replacing the $2,000,000 balance which would have amortized itself in nineteen years. By lengthening the mortgage payments by eleven years, he kept the yearly payments on the new mortgage about the same as they were on the old one. He now was in the enviable position of controlling $2,350,000 worth of apartments with no money of his own, and still continuing to receive a cash flow of $25,000 a year. This is leveraging to infinity. It is getting $25,000 a year with zero investment.

This deal was not made between unequally informed people. Both buyer and seller were astute real estate men. The only difference between them was that the buyer understood and used the leverage principle at the slightest opening, while the seller understood it vaguely, and was not aware of its many ramifications.

The new owner of the 200 apartments, if he wanted to, could get $250,000 cash for his equity above the new $2,350,-000 mortgage. It would be all profit. What happened was that the seller handed my friend $250,000 on a silver platter by not using the leverage principle. The seller made a profit on the sale, but not the top profit layer that comes from leveraging.

Don't get locked into mortgage terms that lock you out of leverage

I own a medical building with a gross income of $250,000 which has a cash flow of $60,000. Capitalizing the $60,000 overage at 10 per cent, I could sell the building for $600,000 above its $800,000 first mortgage balance.

It is the same building I described in Chapter Two, where obtaining financing proved almost insurmountable because I had no tenants when I applied for the loan. When I finally did place an $850,000 mortgage, I was put in a double bind. It called for a 6¼ per cent interest rate, and no payoff privileges the first ten years. I was so eager and grateful to get the loan that I didn't mind the high interest rate, but I should have objected to being locked in a loan for half its life. If I had protested, and arranged for a reasonable payoff penalty, I could have been $200,000 ahead today. It was a small slip that cost a lot of money. Here is why.

Because the building was eventually leased 100 per cent to a fine grade of tenants, I would have no problem getting a new million dollar loan for twenty-five years at 5½ per cent. The yearly interest and principal amortization on such a loan would be approximately the same as the locked-in interest and principal amortization on the $800,000 mortgage balance. The $60,000 cash flow would remain the same even though the mortgage differed by $200,000. Lengthening the mortgage amortization and lowering the interest rate, of course, is what kept the mortgage payments on the new $1,000,000 loan the same as they were on the $800,000 balance. By capitalizing the intact $60,000 cash flow at 10 per cent, I could still sell the building for $600,000 above the new $1,000,000 mortgage, and keep the $200,000 proceeds from the refinancing.

The lesson of this experience is: don't get caught in a mortgage that does not contain a reasonable pay-off clause. Agree to a stiff termination penalty if you have to, but don't agree to no pay-off at all. One never knows when a leveraging opportunity will present itself. Being unable to take advantage of it may prove too costly.

The leverage concept had not yet crystallized in my mind when I signed the $850,000 mortgage on the medical building. Perhaps that's why I was careless in allowing the no termination clause to creep into the terms. I don't intend to make that mistake again, and with my experience as an example, you shouldn't make it either.

Benefits of leverage

Real estate leverage benefits many people—the entrepreneurs, the money lenders and the wage earners. It promotes industrial growth and creates real estate wealth.

Who is more likely to build a million dollar building, one who has a million dollars or one who has $100,000? Nine chances out of ten it will be the one with the $100,000 because there is more excitement and intrigue in creating a lot with a little. We have been conditioned to do things with other people's money. The chances are that the owner of a million dollars would either play it safe and do nothing, or would build a five or ten million dollar building. One of the blessings of our debt economy is that it encourages people to multiply wealth through the technique of responsible borrowing.

An enterpriser who cautiously invests his $100,000 to build a free and clear twelve-family apartment building may be protecting himself, but he is not helping others as much as the entrepreneur who uses the $100,000 to build a million dollar project.

The leverage idea has induced a swarm of brainy people to build real estate projects because of the fantastically high returns resulting from its use. Well conceived and well executed projects often bring as high as 20 per cent and 30 per cent return on equity capital. A lecturer in a commercial property clinic I attended related an incident in which an entrepreneur built an office building for seven million dollars, and leased it so favorably that he obtained an eight million dollar mortgage. The speaker went on to say that, measured by every reasonable standard, this eight million dollar mortgage was as safe as many mortgages backed by 20 per cent or 30 per cent in equity money. The soundness of a mortgage is not dependent upon how much money the entrepreneur puts into the project, but upon an operating statement, the financial caliber of the tenants, and the length of their leases.

The leverage principle has been responsible for putting billions of dollars to work. Insurance companies, building and loan associations, banks and pension funds would be bulging with billions of unused dollars had it not been for the imaginative entrepreneurs who dreamed up the projects and put the money of these big lending institutions to creative uses. Companies in the lending business would not have grown nearly so fast without the leverage principle. Millions of small investors would not have been able to invest as much of their money at 4 per cent to 4½ per cent in savings and loan associations, had it not been for the leverage principle. Pension funds would have less money to distribute to their pensioners if they invested it in government bonds, instead of higher yielding real estate mortgages. Insurance companies would show smaller profits in their investment portfolios if they did not contain billions of dollars worth of high interest-paying mortgages.

The leverage principle fills empty hands with work. Using the leverage principle, I was able to create ten million dollars worth of new real estate wealth, and millions of man hours of construction work. Architects, financiers, investors, contractors and wage earners not only benefited in earnings, but equally as important, were afforded an opportunity to express their skills. I, of course, benefited financially, but, in addition, received a much higher reward—the exhilaration of being creative. I could not have had these absorbing experiences without leverage.

Ideas create wealth. The leverage idea creates the momentum that gets men on the move. It prompts the architect to dream dreams; moves the financier to take risks; creates a market for brick, lumber and steel, and makes demands on the skills of men. And as men are motivated to coordinate these elements, buildings are built and the needs of people are met. Without the leverage principle much of the real estate activity around us would not be taking place.

The underdeveloped countries are slow to progress, not because they don't have the raw materials, but because they don't have the men with ideas to convert them into usable goods. You can have raw materials, and even skills in abundance, and yet, without a catalytic idea like leverage, the optimum is seldom realized. Ideas breathe life into potentiality, and make it reality.

Disadvantages of leverage

Any financially dynamic idea has built-in dangers. The leverage principle, under certain circumstances, can become highly volatile. Owners of thin equities can be wiped out quickly by poor management, or by a minor economic recession. Leveraged projects are so delicately balanced between income and expense that a 10 per cent drop in occupancy can put many of them in the red. For instance, one prolonged vacancy in a highly leveraged four-family apartment ripens it for foreclosure. Or you might be the proud owner of a 100 per cent occupied office building today and be in the red tomorrow because a competitor has weaned away a lucrative tenant with more unique amenities.

One who owns a building free and clear can weather most economic hurricanes. The owner of a finely leveraged building, however, can be blown off his perch by any strong breeze. Leveraging in real estate means living dangerously. Walking a tightrope delicately strung between income and expense is not recommended for the faint-hearted.

The leverage principle attracts some unsound promoters who start unsound projects. Evaluators of real estate loans are often frustrated in trying to separate feasible from unfeasible projects, and deciding who is a loose promoter and who is a genuine entrepreneur. For the unsound men sometimes come up with feasible projects, and the sound men at times propose the ones that seem as safe as a stroll through quicksand. Five lending agencies refused to grant me what I considered a safe $500,000 loan for a senior citizens project. Their loan officers reasoned that elderly people did not have sufficient incomes to pay rent. They blithely placed their money on four-family flats, and in a few years foreclosed many of them.

Let me point to several projects to underscore some of the weaknesses of the leverage principle. It's possible for entrepreneurs, lenders and mortgage insurers, private or governmental, to gloss over facts, use poor judgment, and wind up building white elephants.

A builder I know leveraged a $1,500,000 nursing home to infinity. That is, he built it for the mortgage. But he was confronted with a $200,000 loss the first year of operation. The lender, realizing he had made a mistake, took the rap that year by not getting a dime of interest or principal on his loan. The owner averaged 50 per cent occupancy and was only able to meet his fixed expenses. The mortgagee had no alternative but to "baby" his soft loan, because foreclosure would have been worse. Knowing the owner as well as the lender, and having seen the nursing home, I can only conclude that they must have mesmerized each other. The empty rooms, in an out-of-the-way location, were silent evidence that both entrepreneur and financier had made serious miscalculations. The leverage principle was given a black eye.

In this convalescent home venture, a builder and lender lulled each other into a weak deal and a sick loan. But their errors were small compared to a leveraged 150 garden apartment project, where the glaring mistakes of the builder and the lender were underwritten by the FHA!

In the mid-1950's, the garden apartment project was built and mortgaged for $1,000,000. Ten years later, it was foreclosed and put on the market at $600,000. Why such a loss? Because the project was carelessly built for the immediate "buck" and promoted to bring maximum rents.

The location was excellent. The apartments were near a beautiful park, public transportation and shopping. But construction was shabby, and room layout worse. At the time of foreclosure, most of the foundations were buckling, the asphalt-tile-covered floors were slanting, and the plaster was cracking. In a garden apartment, one has a right to expect spaciousness, yet the builder, lender and mortgage insurer were content with kitchens that were 6 by 8 feet, bedrooms 10 by 11 feet, and with living rooms not much larger than the bedrooms. Beyond shelter, there were no amenities of any kind. No wonder the project failed. A financial tool is as good as the raw material with which it has to work. If the ingredients that go into the deal are poor, the leverage principle accentuates them. You can't make a good omelet out of bad eggs.

A sophisticated leverager I know built 150 apartments without money of his own. Out of pride or morality, I don't know which, he refused to give up, and kept on making up deficits for five years. The project was well conceived and excellently built, the rooms were spacious and tastefully designed. Why was it failing? Because he built too many apartments of the same kind and size for his out-of-the-way location to absorb. To compound his problem, there were another one hundred similarly constructed apartments several blocks away. It was like trying to sell snow in Alaska. There were too many apartments for the neighborhood. Instead of putting in money at the inception of the deal, the entrepreneur was investing it yearly by making up the losses.

Several owners of small office buildings were joyfully rubbing their hands when they "mortgaged out" their buildings 100 per cent, and filled them with five year tenants. At the lease terminations, when 20 per cent to 30 per cent vacancies developed, they had to "take money from home." They had to reach into their own pockets to make up the deficits. To leverage is to live on a knife's edge. One day you're in the black, and the next in the red. And with the scarcity of tenants because of over-building, the red may last a long time—long enough to change owners.

When a shopping center is leveraged to the hilt, and an owner has to maintain a high occupancy rate at high rentals to meet soaring costs, intense conflicts develop between landlord and tenants. Conflicts of survival!

A small greeting card businessman was sold into paying $7 a square foot for space in a regional shopping center, and lost $30,000 in five years because he was carried away by the glitter of potential profits resulting from his location next to a large department store. A woman's apparel shop was heading for bankruptcy in the same center because it couldn't pay the high rents called for in the lease. Yet, the developers were forced to seek business-breaking rents because of the high interest and principal payments in a highly leveraged project. It's a triple-joined battle between tenants, landlord and lender. It's a far cry from the "good old days" when seldom were obligations keyed to such a high leverage pitch.

Yet, without the leverage principle, a former salesman of mine could not have catapulted himself into owning twenty-five million dollars worth of real estate. How did he do it? By buying commercial buildings that had failed because of high leverage and poor occupancy, and putting them back on their feet through imaginative remodeling and leasing. The mortgages he obtained after breathing new life into the buildings were usually more than he paid for the properties.

To quicken the pace of his empire building, my former protégé salesman bought a large contracting firm and began constructing apartments, office buildings, hotels and dormitories for his own investment portfolio. In addition to the usual leveraging maneuvers, he added an extra layer of profit from his contracting operations, so that when a project was completed, money came in instead of going out. He leveraged beyond infinity.

What can happen to an empire that grows like Topsy? It depends on the man and the times. An emotional jar or an economic tremor could send it spinning topsy-turvy. Or it could be the foundation for a family fortune.

The leverage philosophy is built on runaway optimism, and will be severely tested in the event of prolonged economic dislocation. Flippant conclusions of those who can only see through rose colored glasses could saddle the future with a debt load that would be too burdensome for posterity to bear. It comes down to the basic question of differentiating between responsible growth and irresponsible promotion.

What's the answer? Let's see.

How leverage can be used constructively

Obviously, the best way to make use of the leverage principle is to eliminate its weaknesses and concentrate on its strengths. It should be used only in sound ventures that meet the needs of people. To leverage a new office building in a community that has, let's say, a 20 per cent vacancy is financially dangerous and irresponsible. A persuasive entrepreneur who talks a naïve lender into a high percentage loan to compete against 80 per cent occupied office buildings is only undermining the economic foundations of the office building market in his community. Such reckless planning turns normal dealing into cutthroat competition.

It is just as foolhardy for a lending institution to offer attractive mortgage terms on four-family flats when the market is surfeited with them. Nor is the leverage principle used constructively when an entrepreneur persuades a lending institution to give him a high leverage loan for a shopping center that would compete with another that already adequately meets the people's needs. In the long run, it is not good business to apply creative energies where needs already are being met—just because it is easy to borrow money. Instead, pour energies in areas of unmet needs where financing may be more difficult to get. That's where you should use your persuasive ingenuity to leverage to the hilt. That's where leveraging makes the most sense, and brings the best results.

Pioneer in re-zoning attractive neighborhoods for luxury apartments and you'll have a fertile field for high percentage mortgaging. The need for luxury apartments in middle sized cities is just beginning to be met—that's where creative leveraging can have a heyday.

Close to twenty million people in our country are over sixty-five years old. It will take ten years to fulfill the housing needs of these deserving people. What an opportunity for creative leveraging! And what an opportunity to genuinely help older people by taking them out of congested rooming houses, noisy apartments and homes that are too large and lonely! Remember, their rent is as good as the United States government—their pensions and Social Security payments are a better guarantee than that of the largest corporation. Why not educate the lender by pointing out to him the rental security of the elderly and leverage the needed housing for senior citizens to the limit?

Why risk time and reputation to build office buildings and shopping centers which force you into fierce and rapacious competition, when you can, with the aid of government, tackle the problems of slum clearance and urban renewal? That's where the need is now, and where fortunes will be made. That's where the imagination of private enterprise must match the incentives of government.

We have enough office buildings and shopping centers, we have barely begun to clear the slums and renew our cities. That's where leverage should be applied. That's where it's needed!

Why buck a glutted market in in-town apartments, when you can build Wildwood Villages in wooded groves at the edges of most American cities? Build something unique which satisfies people, and you add value to a project beyond its cost of reproduction. The X factor which originality imparts to a real estate venture can be leveraged for an extra 10 per cent to 20 per cent.

Don't build a motor hotel unless you are assured of such

business generators as a hospital, a large industrial complex, or a university center. And don't build another, if one is already there. Why knock each other out?

Borrowing money is a vehicle for progress, if it is used to fill unmet needs. Amortizing a loan over the life of a building is a useful financial tool. And the leverage principle, aided by the long amortization technique, offers opportunities to men with vision.

Leverage used discriminately creates wealth and strengthens our country. A mixture of courage, imagination and leverage will rebuild our decaying cities. It cannot be done with a philosophy of financial conservatism. Only bold leverage concepts will clear the slums and build new urban skylines.

10.

How Real Estate Fortunes
Are Made

A real estate fortune cannot be created from the savings of a normal salary, not in one lifetime. Even if one earned $25,000 a year and saved $5,000 of it, it would take several lifetimes to become a millionaire.

Yet one can legitimately build a multi-million dollar real estate fortune in several years, if he knows the short cuts and is willing to take calculated risks. By using the leverage principle, a $50,000-a-year cash flow can be built in a few years, but to build the same yearly income through the long ordinary income route, one would first have to earn a million dollars and invest it at 5 per cent.

Before I help you adjust your sights on that million dollar target, let me offer a word of caution about the disadvantages of wealth and the sometimes painful route to attain it. While there are many advantages in living the life of a millionaire, you can be plagued by just as many disadvantages—often many more. There's something to the Biblical warning that it is easier for a camel to pass through the eye of a needle than for a rich man to get to heaven. It is difficult to hold on to character in the midst of temptations which bedevil men of wealth. Wealth is difficult to handle. It requires wisdom, and those who want to become rich usually do not have the time to become wise.

You don't need great intelligence to become a real estate tycoon. I can assure you, it requires more mental prowess to become a professor of history, literature or mathematics. One of the main prerequisites for becoming a millionaire is an intense desire to become one. Then you must take advantage of the short cuts that are available. Here they are:

The case of the stinking tannery— or, don't let appearances get you off the scent

Wanting to retire, a tannery owner offered to sell his vacant 500,000 square foot plant for $1,500,000. Prospects looked at it, but didn't know what to do with it. A year later the price went down to $1,000,000, and still there was no interest. Wanting to get rid of it once and for all, the tanner offered it for $500,000 with $100,000 down. I decided to look at it at this point.

I was busy in a number of other projects, but the main reason that I muffed the opportunity, as I look back now, was the unbearable stench that permeated the building. Mostly out of courtesy, I suffered uncomplainingly through the hour it took to inspect the building, and I'm sure the broker stayed with me only to return the courtesy.

When I stepped outside, I gratefully gulped in the fresh air, and then said to my companion:

"Ed, this isn't for me."

I didn't realize it, but I was saying good-bye to a million dollars.

An ordinary businessman with less sensitive nostrils but with more courage and imagination bought the building. He hired a chemist who disinfected it so that it smelled as pleasant as a department store perfume counter, and in one year's time he had leased the entire building to some thirty different tenants at forty cents a square foot. The gross income was $200,000 a year.

With the building leased, he had no problem obtaining a $500,000 first mortgage with a fifteen year amortization. Fixed expenses—heat, taxes, insurance and miscellaneous repairs—plus the yearly interest and principal came to approximately $100,-000. This left the owner with $100,000 a year cash flow, in a deal in which he had no money of his own.

Two million dollars in cash invested at 5 per cent would earn no more for this unschooled businessman. It would take the life-time earnings of perhaps five medical specialists, added to the earnings of five top lawyers, to accumulate $2,000,000 after normal taxes and living expenses. Our businessman accumulated its equivalent in one year. Was he not then a multi-millionaire?

The irony of it was that the broker who sold him the building leased all the space for his client. The broker's leasing commission added to his other normal income was a pittance compared to what his client made in the deal. But we must assume that the broker was not interested in becoming a millionaire. His client was.

How legitimately changing normal to long term income can make you a millionaire

Here is a short cut to amassing a real estate fortune which is very little known and very little used. However, it's available to anyone who is ingenious enough to assemble a favorable set of circumstances.

You must find a man over the age of 60 who has a large normal income, and owns real estate free and clear. For instance, I know a 65 year old businessman who owns a 60 year old office building without any mortgages. It nets $100,000 a year of normal taxable income. He also gets $150,000 a year in earnings and dividends from other normal income sources. This man has no heirs to take over and manage his office building, but he is at an age where he wants to slow down and unharness himself from the burden of management.

Here is how a bright young man who is aspiring to become a millionaire can become one. Suggest to the owner that he sell his building to you for $1,000,000 with $5,000 down, and payments on the balance at the rate of $70,000 a year to include 4 per cent interest until paid. This would leave you a cash flow of $30,000 a year, plus the credit of principal amortization. The advantages, if you believe you have the managerial skill to maintain the building's same level of income, are obvious.

The advantages to the seller have to be examined more carefully. What are they? Well, instead of paying $70,000 a year in normal taxes on his $100,000 net rentals, and being left with $30,000 tax free money, he would pay the 25 per cent long term gain on $42,000 principal of the $70,000 yearly payments, or $10,500, leaving a spendable tax free income of $31,500. In addition, he is left with 30 per cent of $28,000 interest on the same $70,000 yearly payment, or $8,400. This gives him a total tax free income of $39,900, or $9,900 per year more than when he owned the property. And, of course, in addition to the financial advantage, the seller enjoys carefree income. He is no longer bothered with management at an age when it becomes a burden.

There are no disadvantages in this deal to anyone. Only the government will be disadvantaged for a while because under this sale it will be receiving $30,000 in taxes from the seller, instead of $70,000 a year when he owned the building, and probably none from the buyer for several years because he will be tax protected by depreciation. However, when the seller dies, the government will come in for its share, and when the buyer sells, it will participate again. No one gets hurt.

The two main ingredients necessary to make this fascinating deal are a wealthy elderly man with no close heirs who owns high income property with a low depreciation base, and a young man of integrity, who has managerial ability, to become the conduit through which ordinary income is converted to capital gain income for the mutual benefit of both. This combination of circumstances is not easy to find, nor, when found, is it easy to convince the elderly businessman. However, this is a once in a lifetime opportunity. It is for the few, not for the many.

An enterprising young man who can put such a deal together can overnight come into an overage of $30,000 a year, and using a 5 per cent capitalization, gets into the same net worth bracket as the man who has invested $600,000 at 5 per cent. It doesn't take too many deals like this to catapult into the millionaire class. I am not writing about "pie in the sky," though it sounds too easy. However, these opportunities exist. If you look for them, you'll find them, and when you learn how to delineate the benefits for the "other guy," you will get results.

How a restaurant manager became its owner and made more in one year than in twenty years of managing

A wealthy department store executive, more as a hobby than for profit, bought a nationally famous restaurant in Milwaukee for $275,000. The price included a Gay Nineties vintage fifty-room hotel. The quality bistro was prominently displayed on the first floor. It was located near the Chicago and Northwestern Railroad Depot. When railroading was in its heyday, the hotel catered to the traveling elite. But now the rooms had lost their elegance. They had deteriorated to rooming house status. The restaurant, however, retained its oldtime atmosphere and prestige.

After several years of bistro hobbying, the department store executive's duties became more pressing, and what had started out as a lark became a burden. He called me one day and said:

"George, I've got to sell the restaurant. It's taking too much of my time."

For half a year, I tried to get the $275,000 he paid for it but there was no interest. He called again, and almost in desperation, said:

"George, I've got to get rid of it. It's no fun anymore. Too many problems."

There is one sure way, I told him, of accelerating the chances of sale, and that is to reduce the price drastically.

"All right," he said, "get me $200,000, but it's got to be all cash. I want to get out of it completely."

Even at the low price, I was unable to find a buyer.

One day while I was eating at his restaurant (and my meal was exceptionally good), I was suddenly struck with an idea. I called the manager to my table and said:

"How would you like to own this building, restaurant and all?"

"What a question!" he said. "Sure I'd like to own it, but how do I do it without money?"

"If you've got a little guts and imagination, I think I can show you how you can own this place, and perhaps some day get started on becoming a millionaire."

Stimulated by the idea born at the dinner table, I zeroed in for action.

"If you don't have any money of your own, can you borrow $25,000 from a friend or relative? If my idea works, you can not only own this building, but because it's part of an important square block, you may strike gold and get a half million dollars for it, if someone decides to develop it."

"All right," he said excitedly, "I don't know what you're talking about, but go ahead, tell me how I can own it. I can borrow $25,000 from my mother."

Within several weeks, I arranged for a $115,000 first mortgage and, after being refused by a half dozen people who specialize in secondary financing, I sold an $80,000 mortgage on the building for $60,000 in cash to the restaurant's wholesale meat dealer. The manager added the $25,000 (borrowed from his mother), paid his ex-employer $200,000 in cash and became the owner. The price to the buyer, of course, was $220,000 because of the $20,000 premium for selling the second mortgage to his meat dealer. The new owner now owed $115,000 on a first mortgage and $80,000 on a second mortgage.

The former manager was floating on pink clouds. He had worked in restaurants all his life, and now at the age of 41 he was not only the owner of his own place, but had a $220,000 building as well. It seemed incredible to him, but what happened a year later was even more improbable.

A group of men decided to build a complex of office buildings, and picked his square block for development. When asked how much he wanted for his building he casually said, $450,000. Would he give them an option? Why not, he thought. A year later he received $450,000 in cash.

It was another one of those "once in a lifetime deals," which can lift an ordinary restaurant manager from just making a living and put him into the wealthy class. Of course, he played his role well. In addition to a favorable set of circumstances, he did have the courage to plunge and, of course, he was lucky. And having a mother who was willing to risk $25,000 of her savings didn't hurt.

The manager of the restaurant would have had to work two lifetimes at $12,000 a year, the salary he was getting, to save what he made in one year, in one real estate deal. It sounds fantastic, but it's true, and it can happen to you.

His pattern was simple, and he became a millionaire

At one of the Commercial Property Clinics which I attend every year in Chicago, I met a bored grandfather who complained that he was no longer getting a "kick" out of his real estate deals.

He said: "My wife and I have more money than we can

possibly use in our remaining years. My two children have trusts in their names to provide amply for them, and I have just finished setting up trusts for my grandchildren. Now, I'm saddened because I don't really have any reason to work."

He was earnestly distressed. He told me that life was exciting only when he was building his real estate empire.

"Now," he continued, "what I do is unreal, it's synthetic."

"Would you mind telling me how you built your fortune?" I asked him at one of the session breaks. "You seem to be a philosopher as well as a practical man. I'd like to get your views on both."

"You know," he said, "our seminar leaders are all fine men, experts in their fields, but I don't think any of them knows how to make a real estate fortune for himself. I'm not a good enough speaker to lecture about it, I only know how to do it.

"Twenty-five years ago, when I was 35, I decided I was too much of an individualist to work for someone else. But more important, I realized that with our tax structure it would take too long to build a fortune running a business which earned normal income. I wanted to make a lot of money in a hurry. The real estate business, as I envisaged using it, could do it.

"I had little money and a great deal of ambition. As I look back, too much ambition. A little ambition is good, too much is bad.

"Here's how I got started. I solicited commercial and industrial tenants and offered to build small buildings for them. 'Don't lose your identity in another building,' I would tell them. 'Enjoy the prestige of your individualized business name.' My clients were insurance companies and small local industrial concerns who needed from 3,000 to 10,000 square feet. I was able to lease these free standing buildings favorably for these reasons. I saw twenty lots before buying the best at the best price. I sublet my mason work, carpentry, electrical, plumbing and heating to small but reliable contractors, who worked on a small profit margin. With ten year leases in hand, I was able to get ten to fifteen year financing. Twenty to thirty year amortization was not available then.

"Even with the faster amortization, I was able to build up cash flows with no investment of my own. I kept putting up five to six buildings a year, and as the amortization rates of loans were lengthened, my cash flow in the buildings increased. In fact, I followed a formula that for every $100,000 of building, I saw to it that I was left with a 3 to 5 per cent cash flow.

"I have built about $4,000,000 worth of buildings which now generate about $200,000 a year cash flow. If I capitalize it at 10 per cent, I suppose that would give me an equity position of $2,000,000, plus what I have paid off on my mortgages. As you can see, I did very well.

"However, as I have grown wealthier, I have also grown wiser. But wisdom disturbs me. For instance, I am seriously questioning the wisdom of providing complete financial security for my children and grandchildren, and thereby robbing them of the tremendous exhilaration one gets in building for himself. I know my children are not getting the 'kick' out of life I did. They're too secure and blasé.

"Another thing bothers me. I honestly must confess that I enjoyed making money much more than giving it away. I give as much as anyone to the usual charities. My problem, however, is that I get no kick out of giving. In fact, when a solicitor for a charitable cause rubs me the wrong way, I can easily turn against him and his cause. I know that's shallow thinking, but I can't help it.

"I have been unable to convert the money making enthusiasm I had fifteen years ago into inspired living. Perhaps there is more zest at the end of the trail for a $25,000 a year man, than for a millionaire like me?"

It's exhilarating to become a millionaire, and as this real estate philosopher points out, it's not difficult to become one.

What's more difficult is to develop a sense of fulfillment—of finding something big to live for.

I learn a million dollar lesson

After World War II, when it was difficult to predict where the swirling economic currents would take us, I was offered one of those "it can only happen once" deals. Had I read somewhere what I'm trying to convey in this chapter, I would have had no problem making the right decision, and would not have allowed $1,000,000 to slip through my fingers.

My hope is that after you read of my error, you will not make the same mistake.

The Mitchell Mackie office building is a charming landmark in Milwaukee. To the connoisseur, its architecture conveys the elegance of the old world, but to the layman it appeared to be nothing more than a dirty gray brick building with lots of gingerbread. It had 100,000 square feet of space, and was about eighty years old.

A smart entrepreneur saw its possibilities and bought it for somewhere in the $100,000 to $150,000 range. He was a speculator, not a creator. He was not interested in remodeling, leasing, or managing. He came to me.

"George," he said, "I want a trouble free investment. You're a remodeler. You know how to lease and manage. You've done it successfully on a small scale. If you're ready for a big one, I'd like to lease the Mitchell Mackie Building to you for fifty years at $25,000 a year, net to me. If you can do with this building what you've done with others, you can rent it for $300,000 a year."

His analysis was correct. There was only one hitch. He wanted a security deposit of $100,000. I told him I didn't have the cash. His mind, racing ahead of mine, concocted a very creative suggestion.

"I happen to know that you have a twelve-family apartment building on Wisconsin Avenue that is free and clear. Give it to me as security under the following conditions: You continue to own, manage and keep the income from it, but you cannot mortgage it, or sell it; in the event you cannot meet the $25,-000 yearly payments, you must either mortgage or sell your building, and use all the proceeds to satisfy your obligations to me. This is the general idea. Our lawyers can nail it down more specifically."

At the time, the Wisconsin Avenue apartment building was all the security I had. My sights were low then, and the $8,000 a year net income looked enchantingly good. The leverage philosophy never entered my mind in those days. For several weeks I went through agonizing indecision. I wanted to hold on to my security, but I wanted to build a real estate fortune, too. My conservatism won out, and I lost a million dollars.

Within several months, the speculator sold the building for $400,000. The new owner cancelled all the existing leases, remodeled the building and leased its space at $3 a square foot. Within three years his building had an income of $300,000 a year, and a market value of $1,500,000.

Muffing this deal taught me a valuable lesson. You cannot build a real estate fortune with a faint heart. If you want something, you must risk something—whether it's work or something tangible you own. As I look back, I realize how naïve I was. I froze into a conservatism that went beyond reason. There I was at 35, more concerned about security than about the opportunity offered me. My mind wasn't tuned to building a real estate fortune. When one becomes more interested in security than in making a lot of money, it is exceedingly difficult to become a millionaire.

I didn't make the same mistake again. The deal taught me a million dollar lesson. In the years that followed, I took

longer chances for far smaller rewards. But never again did I
have the opportunity to make so much and risk so little.

Making a fortune in land

There are many facetious stories about men who, had they
learned how to read and write and gotten good jobs, would
never have become empire builders. I know one unschooled
millionaire who quipped that if he had gone to college he
couldn't have afforded the expensive college graduates who
were on his payroll.

Native intelligence with lots of go behind it, unleashed during periods of opportunity, has more dynamism than schooled
knowledge carefully directed.

Many of the men who made fortunes in developing land in
the 1950's and 1960's were unsuccessful or mediocre in other
lines of work, and with unbounded desire reached out to overcome their deficiencies by taking long chances. I cannot think
of a single land speculator or developer, and I know many of
them, who had either the patience or scholarship required to
master knowledge that needed careful and orderly concen-
tration.

Developing land brings a quick half million

I know two brothers who were several years apart. The older
one went on to become a skilled surgeon. The other barely got
through high school, and then bounced aimlessly from failure
to failure, searching for "the big break" to set him up for the
"killing."

He found it in land development. Gambling on information
that sewer and water service was to be extended in a certain
direction, he optioned a 120 acre tract of land in the path of
the projected utilities. He had no money of his own, but was
able to persuade a businessman friend to advance $50,000 of

the $150,000 purchase price, on the basis that he would do all of the subdividing work, and split the profit with his "angel." Within eighteen months they divided $300,000. He was on his way.

At 35, the older brother was slowly building his medical practice, driving a Chevrolet and living in a $150 a month apartment, while at 32 his kid brother was driving a Cadillac and living in a $40,000 home.

A successful deal charges an ambitious man with confidence. Our young hero became supercharged. He dug in on his success with bulldog tenacity, and working seventy hours a week developed subdivision after subdivision until he built a fortune of half a million dollars.

Then his ambition overran his astuteness. He built thirty $40,000 homes on speculation just as a recession hit the national economy. He could neither sell nor rent them. Within two years he lost most of his fortune—and his health—from nervous exhaustion.

The life of an ambitious entrepreneur is a hard one. If he does not have the emotional resiliency to absorb the shocks of fluctuating fortunes, he is more likely to break than bend. It is easier to amass a fortune than attain serenity.

A lathe operator's secret builds a five million dollar fortune

A lathe operator earning $75 a week was bored with his work and gambled his steady income for the uncertainties of selling real estate on commission. Within a year, when he was 28, he set out on his own. He had little knowledge to guide him. A storm of ambition drove him ahead.

More by accident than by design, he optioned a piece of land, and within several weeks sold it for a $15,000 profit. It was more than he had earned in his three years at the factory.

A surge of excitement ran through him. If he could make $15,000 that easily, the sky would be the limit, and he reached for it.

His appetite for making money was gargantuan. He bit off more deals than he could digest. His secret, however, was to overpay for land he thought was in the path of growth, but in return to demand easy terms. He tied up farms, highway acreage, and busy edge-of-town intersection corners with a few thousand dollars down and an agreement to pay several thousand more in a year or two, and the balance perhaps five years later. This happened in the late 1940's and early 1950's. As land prices began to rise, his farms blossomed into subdivisions, his highway acreage into commercial and apartment sites, and his highway intersections into shopping center locations. The ordinary speculator would have taken short profits and run. Not he! He would sell one or two of the dozens of parcels he had tied up, and with the profits meet his payment obligations on the thousands of acres he had under contract. By the middle 1950's he was sitting on gold mines. The value of his land holdings zoomed.

He was not content to sell at tremendous profits. He developed his holdings himself. He put his secret of overpayment in reverse. He would sell lots to builders at high prices but on easy terms, 10 per cent down and 90 per cent when the homes were sold. He went further. He built a sales organization, and sold these homes for the builders on a commission. This was in addition to building and selling several thousand homes on his own lots, which cost him a pittance compared to the prices he was getting from the builders.

Nor did the hurricane of his ambition stop there. He discovered that when he built subdivisions of homes, the ten- and twenty-acre corners became valuable community shopping center sites. Entrepreneurs excitedly offered fantastic prices for them. Calmly he refused, and built the shopping centers himself.

Raw land for which he paid less than a $1,000 an acre became valuable apartment sites. He was not content to sell these for twenty times what he paid for them, and built hundreds of apartments for his own investment portfolio.

Remnants of subdivisions became valuable locations for office buildings, free standing commercial stores and discount houses. He built some of these buildings himself, and leased land to others, instead of selling it—for good tax reasons.

In 1960, at 43, our lathe operator found himself drained of energy. He was emotionally and physically exhausted. His doctors advised him to stop wheeling and dealing, liquidate his empire, and move to a warm climate. Reluctantly but wisely he did. I see him now and then when he comes to visit Milwaukee, a lot calmer than when I dueled with him on deals, and with the confidence of a five million dollar fortune behind him.

Those who will want to get doctors degrees in land economics will calmly dissect and evaluate what our lathe operator did in the heat of a decade. They will assemble, interpret and collate his ventures into principles of land economics. The professors and their students will probably understand this pedagogy better than the lathe operator would—if he ever took time to read it. But they will not have in their texts a description of the learning process where the chief guide is trial by fire and error. The scholars, away from the emotional turbulence that is the natural habitat of rampant ambition, cannot describe its driving force, unless they sit alongside a pulsating entrepreneur and wince at his antics and tactics.

The professor, the good lawyer, or the astute businessman is too busy being successful to plunge into land development. Usually the opportunities fall into the lap of the lathe operator type, who, being unsuccessful, has nothing to lose, and, being ambitious, takes long chances. Having native intelligence, he learns quickly. If, added to these, he develops a burning desire to become rich and the economic cycle is in his favor, he blossoms into a multimillionaire.

If you don't learn while you earn you can't become a millionaire

A young friend of mine dropped out of college because he was more interested in earning than learning. He stumbled onto a pot of gold the first year after he received his real estate broker's license. He obtained an option on forty acres of land owned by a fairly knowledgeable land developer. Within several weeks, one of the area's most successful dealers offered my young friend $50,000 profit for his land. He was dumbfounded. He had no idea why the land was worth $50,000 more than his option called for. Fearing that his buyer saw something that he couldn't see, and wanting to squeeze all he could out of the deal, he came to me for advice.

"What do I do?" he asked. "Should I take the profit, or try to develop the land myself, and go for broke?"

I was flabbergasted to see my neophyte friend even hesitating. I advised him to grab his $50,000.

"Get a few of these deals under your belt before you decide to go for broke," I said.

He took my advice and the $50,000 profit.

But he didn't have the stuff millionaires are made of. He flitted between land speculators and developers, trusting more to luck than knowledge. Soon he lost most of his profit on options that didn't materialize into deals. He didn't realize that once one gets on the track where the big money is, he must learn quickly and move fast.

While his competitors were cramming facts down their ambitious gullets, figuring angles and sharpening their astuteness, my young friend relied on chance to get him into big time. While those who started with him in the land developing business earned their "doctor degrees" in two or three action packed years, he had still not learned the high school lessons. He lost his stride, and after a few years got out of the real estate race altogether. He is now selling Cadillacs to the men who "came in."

They turned land development into a science

This is a Horatio Alger story of two brothers-in-law, one an insurance agent and the other a draftsman. If each had been successful in his field, there would be nothing to tell. But they were only average, and because they were, they became millionaires—in land development.

After a few minor successes, they found a simple key to an unbelievable potential in land development. And instead of going about unlocking this door to fortune haphazardly, the way my young friend did several pages back, they rolled up their sleeves and went to work methodically.

They put their eyes and noses into City Hall committee activities that dealt with extending water mains and sewer lines into undeveloped land areas. Few people took the time to find out where public utilities were expanding one year, two years, or three years hence. They did, and it paid off.

They bought tracts of land in the path of the planned water and sewer mains for $500 an acre in the early 1950's, just as Milwaukee was about to experience a decade of unprecedented expansion. Other land speculators did the same, but could not resist the temptation to resell them at $1,000 to $2,000 an acre a few years later. But not the brothers-in-law! They turned down $5,000 an acre! They subdivided the land themselves, and made that extra layer of profit.

They didn't stop there. They formed a building company,

and built several hundred homes a year on their own subdivided lots, and made $1,500 profit on each home, which was a sort of frosting on the cake.

Each brother-in-law became a multi-millionaire. They saw the land development of the future, and rode out its crest. They started in time and quit in time.

If they were asked to write an article, or give a speech explaining how they attained their success, their efforts might leave much to be desired. But in eyeball to eyeball confrontation, they knew where the treasure was. They knew their business, they knew what they wanted, and the favorable land development cycle did the rest.

Building apartments—the way to a real estate fortune

One of the surest ways to join the millionaire class is to build fifty new apartments a year for ten years. It takes little money to do this, if one picks the locations imaginatively, designs special amenities that appeal to tenants, and finances them with leverage know-how. It's being done in many American cities. I know two young men who are doing it in Milwaukee.

John and Jerry were each 27 years old when they had to decide whether to continue building and selling homes, activities that were netting their partnership $30,000 a year of ordinary income, or tighten their belts, forget about immediate income, and build apartments. Their instincts were those of fortune hunters, and they followed them.

They had youth—that was an important start. Using good judgment they held on to their partnership because intuitively they knew they needed each other. John was mechanically inclined and gifted with the ability to produce quality apartments at low prices. Jerry knew little about construction but excelled in "smelling out" good locations, buying them right, opening doors at City Hall and closing loans that required little "money from home." They were ideally matched.

Without ever reading or hearing about leverage, they in-
~tinctively put it into practice. Their master plan to become
millionaires was clearly blueprinted in their minds. I talked to
one of the partners about their decision five years later, and he
was as definite about his goal to become a millionaire as a
medical student is of becoming a doctor.

He said, "Each of us is 32 years old and we are already on
our way. We own 300 apartments. In five years, we'll own 600.
We may quit then, or perhaps go for 1,000. I don't know. If we
go for 1,000 apartments we'll own $10,000,000 worth of real
estate. We'll surely quit then. By the time we're 55, if the economy remains about the same, we'll both be millionaires. That's
our goal."

They started with a long-range ambition, and are far along
their way to realizing it. Neither of the partners excelled in
scholarship. It was not their forte. The Phi Beta Kappas and
honor students of their day went on to get the top jobs in industry. Not John and Jerry—they weren't picked.

Rarely do the scholars become millionaires—they're too
smart. The ordinary ones have a better chance.

Systematic buying of apartments can lead to a fortune

Buying existing apartments is a variation of the building-
new-apartments theme, and can lead to the same successful
results.

Jack is a young attorney who was too impatient to wait for
the occasional fees that came from his practice. He was less
than average as a lawyer but had more than average ambition
to amass a fortune.

A real estate broker told him about a twelve-family apartment building which the owner wanted to sell in a hurry Jack
knew a secretary of a savings and loan association that happened to have more idle money than loans. Jack obtained a
mortgage equal to what he paid for the twelve-family. After

he made a few changes in the apartments and raised the rents, he built a cash flow of $3,000 a year. It was half what he had been earning in a year of law practice. Quite by accident he took the first step toward becoming a millionaire.

Within several years, Jack owned one hundred apartments His cash flow was $15,000 a year. He spent half his time looking for buys and managing his properties, and the other half practicing law. One day I said to him:

"Jack, do you want to be a lawyer or a millionaire?"

"A millionaire, of course." he said quickly.

"Then you're going about it the wrong way. For instance, how many properties do you see a week with the ultimate purpose of adding them to your investment portfolio?"

"One or two," he answered.

"If you want to get into the business of buying apartments, you've got to see ten to twenty. And if you don't have enough money to buy all those that look good, sell a half interest in some to investors who are willing to put up all the money."

Jack suddenly looked at me with an expression which seemed to say, "I've been thinking about this myself, but now hearing you say it, I'm going to do it."

"You know," he said, "I've been reluctant to let go of my law practice because of pride. But it doesn't make economic sense. I'm no great lawyer. My heart's not in it. But I'm pretty good at acquiring and managing property—in fact good enough to become a millionaire, if I take your advice and go all the way."

What started with an accidental purchase of a twelve-family apartment building resulted in a plan to build a fortune. He now spends ten hours a day looking at apartment buildings, analyzing statements and making offers. His only overhead is a two room office and a secretary. When I saw him several years later he owned two hundred apartments. His aim was to build his investment portfolio to 500, and then semi-retire into managing them. There is nothing to stop him from realizing his plans except an economic depression.

Jack has the temperament of a potential millionaire. He has inordinate ambition and a calculating mind. The only obstacle that could have stopped him from building a fortune was being a brilliant lawyer. Then he would have stayed in law and done well. But since he was indifferent to law, he did the easier thing. He set out to become a millionaire.

The value of time in the real estate business

The one sure way to build a real estate fortune in one lifetime, or in part of a lifetime, is to buy or build real estate which yields 10 per cent before interest and principal payments, borrow as close to 100 per cent as possible and keep the interest rate below 6 per cent, if possible. The difference between the 10 per cent yield and 6 per cent interest gives one a 4 per cent margin within which to build a fortune. Two per cent of this should be used to amortize principal and 2 per cent for cash flow. This puts time to work for the entrepreneur. He earns 4 per cent, day and night, on all the money he borrows and puts to use. He is only limited by his ability to build or buy buildings which yield 10 per cent. This is not difficult.

This, of course, is the same principle the banks and savings and loan associations use. They borrow money at the lowest interest rate they can, and loan it at the highest interest rate they can get. And the profit margin between what they pay for for money and get in return works for them day and night.

The real estate fortune builder, in fact, has an advantage over the banks and savings and loan associations. They need a lot of capital to get started, while the real estate enterpriser, by using leverage, can do it without money.

There are only a handful of money making fields in which time can be tamed as easily as it can be in real estate. Leverage telescopes time and builds millionaires—in a hurry.

The importance of timing in real estate ventures

The prerequisites for a sense of timing are knowledge, common sense and intuition.

For instance, a women's apparel merchant I know had that sixth sense of timing when he began buying land in one of the Milwaukee suburbs at $50 a front foot. Ten years later, he sold several blocks of it for $500 a front foot. His sense of timing was perfect.

My timing in erecting the Bockl Building in 1956 was one of those happy strokes of intuition. My rationale was that since no new office buildings had gone up in my area for thirty years, the time was ripe for one. My intuition in this one was backed by good common sense.

In 1950, I was offered a forty acre shopping center site for $100,000. I turned it down. Another company bought it, and built the Southgate Shopping Center. It turned out to be a gold mine because the developer's timing was ideal. And, I might ask myself, where was my intuition on this one? Good timing increases the chances for leveraging a project. Favorable timing is what often gives it the margin of success.

Ten per cent of the people in our country are over 65 years. That's nineteen million people. We haven't scratched the surface in meeting their housing needs. Congregate living for the elderly is available to some extent in the South, but it is conspicuously absent in the northern climates. The timing for meeting their needs will never be better than now—when the need is so great.

In the late 1940's and early 1950's, I remodeled loft buildings into office space at low prices. It worked then because there was a need. My timing was right, but remodeling lofts would not be profitable now. Within every major real estate trend there are smaller cycles which sometimes go with the major trend, but often move in opposite directions. If you develop an alertness for these localized trends, and a "feel" for timing them, you reap the rewards of the pathfinding pioneer.

The timing is right for wildwood villages, villages in the sky, leisure clubs, downtown malls, lighted golf courses, urban renewal and congregate housing for the elderly. With billions in the coffers of mortgage institutions waiting for the right projects, and leverage available to keep these funds flowing, the opportunities for imaginative men are unlimited. Many more real estate fortunes will be made in the next twenty-five years than have been made in the last quarter century.

Index

Index